THE NORWICH
CANARY

THE NORWICH CANARY

A Guide to Keeping, Breeding and Showing

JOE BRACEGIRDLE

BLANDFORD

First published in the UK 1988 by **Blandford Press**
An imprint of Cassell
Artillery House, Artillery Row, London SW1P 1RT

Distributed in the United States by
Sterling Publishing Co, Inc,
2 Park Avenue, New York, NY 10016

Distributed in Australia by
Capricorn Link (Australia) Pty Ltd
PO Box 665, Lane Cove, NSW 2066

Bracegirdle, Joe
    The Norwich canary.
    1. Pets: Norwich canaries
    I. Title
    636.6′862

ISBN 0-7137-2019-0

Typeset at the Alden Press Oxford London and Northampton

Printed and bound in Great Britain by
Biddles Ltd, Guildford and King's Lynn

Contents

*May the wing of friendship
never moult a feather*

Acknowledgements

I would like to thank Bill Chilton of Cheadle for allowing me to take photographs of his Norwich canary bird room, equipment, and birds. It was his keen interest in the Norwich canary that persuaded me to write this book.

Preface

It is often said that for anyone new to the fancy, Norwich canaries are very difficult birds with which to commence breeding. What about my early experience with Borders? I first started to breed canaries in May 1935 with two pairs of Borders. At the end of that breeding season I had bred just one young Border from two pairs!

Many of the fanciers who start out with Norwich often experience three or four breeding seasons with poor results. Not surprisingly they cease to keep the birds, saying that they are too difficult a canary from which to breed. This is not the case. All that is needed is for the new fancier to learn first the art of canary breeding. Consequently, I have tried to provide as much detail as possible on how to breed successfully any variety of canary.

My fifty-one years of breeding, exhibiting, judging, writing and lecturing about canaries has taken me round the world four times. It has involved me flying over 150,000 miles with visits to Eire, Spain, Malaysia, Singapore, Australia (in 1978, 1980, 1982 and 1987) and the USA. I have judged canaries at the national shows of England, Spain, Australia and the USA – being the only non-American fancier to have done so.

I hope that readers will forgive my use of 'he' when referring to breeders or fanciers. While overseas it has been my good fortune to have met many very knowledgeable lady canary fanciers and judges, but in the UK there are only a few; why is this so?

May I wish all Norwich fanciers success with their chosen hobby, and much pleasure and enjoyment in visiting shows, bird rooms, canary clubs, and the making of life-long friendships.

Joe Bracegirdle
Cheadle, Cheshire
1988

1
History, Background and Basic Principles

The Norwich canary was first introduced into England by Flemish refugees nearly four hundred years ago. The refugees fled their native homeland in the seventeenth century because of persecution by the Spanish. They landed in Norfolk, settling in and around Norwich, where Flemish-born people were already established. These refugees brought with them not only their working skills but also their pet canaries, which – as time went by – they started to breed. Canary breeding had already spread to most parts of Germany as well as extensively in the Netherlands. By the early nineteenth century, the former refugees and their strange new canary were well established and accepted by the local people in England – so much so that many of the natives had begun to keep and to breed the Flemish type of canary. As the centre of these activities was the town of Norwich, over a period of time the canary took on the name of the Norwich canary.

In those far-away years, the Norwich canary (as the illustration on p. 10 shows) was of a very much slimmer outline than the Norwich we know today. At the beginning of the nineteenth century, all the canaries were small and slim, and many were heavily variegated. The Norwich canary of today is often referred to as the 'John Bull' of the fancy. This change or evolution in the Norwich has been caused by generations of dedicated and knowledgeable breeding by canary fanciers. It has taken some two hundred years to reach today's type of Norwich, which is accepted by canary breeders all over the world.

The first specialist Norwich canary society was formed in 1901, and was called the Norwich Plainhead Club (NPC), which is still very active today. Other specialist clubs came long after. I have a very old canary book that clearly states that as far back as 1880, there were forty or more entries of classes of Norwich canaries at shows. In those days the birds were mostly variegated – the beautiful clear Norwich we now see so often had not yet evolved.

The outstanding beauty and colour of a Norwich canary owes much to the skill of the fancier who has colour fed his birds before and during the moulting period. The practice of colour feeding a canary is to enhance or improve a bird's own natural colour. It was evolved by European breeders, and the practice dates back to the late eighteenth century. However, it was only during the nineteenth century that

A very early type of Norwich, similar to an Australian Plainhead

English fanciers first took up this practice. The following remarks will explain the present methods used by most UK fanciers when colour feeding their birds.

COLOUR FEEDING

In the mid-nineteenth century, European breeders colour fed their canaries by using cayenne pepper mixed in the soft food and drinking water. For those fanciers who are new to the fancy, the following types of canaries have to be colour fed before they can be exhibited: Norwich, Yorkshire, Lizard and New Colours. This is done by feeding them with a colouring agent, such as carophyll red powder mixed with both their drinking water and soft food, giving it to all these canaries four or five weeks before the birds commence their moult, and continuing to feed them with it until the end of the show season. The purpose of colour feeding is to enhance the canary's own natural colour. The difficult thing to achieve is a depth of colour with evenness throughout the feathers. Care must be taken not to colour feed the white-ground Norwich.

Colour feeding is *not* permitted in any of the following varieties: Borders, Glosters, Fifes, Crests, Rollers and all Old Variety canaries.

Green seeding dock, excellent feed for all moulting canaries

These have to be bred for their natural depth of colour, and this can only be helped by feeding natural green foods and wild seeds – one of the most helpful being the green seeding dock.

When a canary drinks or eats anything containing carophyll red, its digestive system passes it into the blood stream, which in turn carries it to all parts of the bird's body and so into the tiny growing feather quills. This is why you must be careful always to use the same quantity of colour feed; otherwise your birds will moult out an uneven shade of colour. Some fanciers sprinkle colour powder lightly over soaked or sprouted seed, stirring it together with a fork before feeding it to their birds. Other fanciers crush rape seed with a fine fork, sprinkle it with colour powder, stir it together, and then feed it. The reason I recommend the use of carophyll red as a colouring agent is that it is water soluble and can therefore be used with both soft food and drinking water. When using it with soft food I suggest you use a heaped teaspoonful of powder, 3 to 4 g to 1.5 kg of dry soft food, mixing it thoroughly together with a fork before adding any form of moisture – be it hard-boiled egg passed through a fine sieve or water. Because of the colouring strength of carophyll red, it is only necessary to use small quantities of it. If an alternative is used in either drinking water or as a moistener for the soft food, it is very difficult to ensure the same strength of solution is mixed with your daily feed or drink. The powder form is a far more effective way to ensure the same daily strength of mixture. The colouring agent *must* be used every day until the birds have completed their full moult, then given two or three times a week until the end of the show season. This will ensure that any feathers that might be accidentally lost after the moult will – on growing again – attain the same shade of colour, and so not adversely affect your showing the bird again. When colour-fed canaries are in moult they should be given fresh carrot and sliced red peppers daily. All these show canaries should be caged on their own. This not only keeps them nice and steady, but also ensures their feathers remain in immaculate condition, especially if they are given a shallow bath of water twice a week.

It is very important to appreciate from the start that in breeding Norwich canaries you must only pair a yellow bird to a buff bird. It does not matter too much which of the pair is the cock or the hen – the first objective is to ensure good feather production in the young you breed. The buff bird should have close, compact feathers, the yellow silkiness of texture and colour. This pairing-up arrangement should only be abandoned when specific results are required by an experienced breeder. One reason for so doing might be if you had a buff bird of very good type and wing carriage, but that had a very 'thin' feather. You would then pair it up to another buff that excelled in its feather. You might pair two yellows to obtain the opposite effect. However, this must only be done for one or two generations, until the required feather texture has been obtained.

In the case of double buffing, a buff can be selected to pair with birds that have been double buffed, bred from yellow and buff, if it is found necessary to double buff more than one breeding season in succession. By so doing, undue sacrifice of colour and silkiness of texture in the feather is avoided. There could be other reasons for this pairing, but it must be understood that the rule – as applied to feather – is: pairing of two yellows induces thinness, the pairing of two buffs having the opposite effect.

It will be readily realised that the breeder must exercise a considerable amount of genetical skill in order to reach the very high standards of today's exhibition Norwich. The breeder must set out to maintain at all times the variety's perfection of feather quality and its depth and evenness of colour. This illustrates the difference between breeding exhibition canaries and poultry.

A fancier has to contend with two types of feather in canaries, which have to be kept balanced whilst at the same time mixed to maintain both feather 'surface' and 'grain'. This is what makes the breeding of a top exhibition canary so difficult. This is just one of several features Norwich fanciers have to understand before they can expect to become skilled breeders – both to attain and to maintain this balance of quality of feather. While we are busy endeavouring to reproduce this feather quality, the breeder must also endeavour to keep, or even improve, the finish of the feather responsible for the bird's colour. This can only be done by first ensuring that the qualities we are trying to achieve are already being carried by *both* our breeding pair. This is not always easy to do, as perhaps one of our pair of birds does not readily show this feature. Even so, it can possess dominant genes that will produce the feature quality required in the young.

Only breed from a stud of birds that readily reproduce the desired feather quality. This also very much includes *all* the out crosses you bring into your bird room. Fanciers must also ensure that they pair up a buff bird to a yellow bird, and in so doing maintain the essential link that goes to breed outstanding exhibition birds. It is this careful balancing of buff to yellow that is the key link to the reproduction of quality of feather. However, it is not just a matter of automatically pairing up buff to yellow that reproduces quality of feather in the young – it is equally important that both pairs of birds carry dominant genes for reproducing quality of feather that has also depth of natural colour.

The gene for reproducing a natural depth of colour comes, without doubt, from the yellow bird. This does not mean that a buff bird does not carry *and* show a great purity of its natural colour, but we do see some buffs that display a complete lack of depth of natural colour. This is the reason a fancier sometimes pairs up two yellows, the next breeding season pairing up the double-yellowed birds to buffs. The philosophy of this is nothing more than a concentration into one channel of the possibility to produce the yellow factor. This is generally only done where the previous pairing has been buff to buff for one, or even two, generations. When doing this, great care must be taken that the young bred in this way do not have the feather's lustre dimmed by an appearance of mealiness – which some birds show. Where it does occur, the pairing of double yellows – i.e. the young bred from two yellows – showing this extra population of buff blood, restores the proper balance of colour.

We must not forget that the colours yellow and buff are each controlled by a single gene, which is produced when mating occurs between a pair of birds. If a pair of birds, each of which is a yellow, is mated together, then you would expect their resultant young also to be yellows. However, it is possible for Nature to have given one of the birds a buff factor or gene. When such birds are bred, they have a very good depth of colour, and are useful birds to breed from. Should you be fortunate enough to breed a young buff cock in this way, then providing he is good in type he can be paired to several yellow hens the next breeding season. Their resultant young should have excellent colour.

THE VALUE OF GREENS

Assuming that your aim is to breed clear exhibition-quality birds, your first question will be, how is it done? You may already have one or two birds that are not completely clear but that are very good for both type and quality of feather. By all means retain these birds and pair them to a completely clear bird that also has a clear flue, feathers, beak, and legs. By pairing either a ticked or variegated bird to a completely clear bird you should achieve two important aims: to breed some completely clear birds; and maintain that very important depth of colour. This being so, you will have proved in just one breeding season how to breed clears that have feathering with the distinctive colour. The genes your marked breeding bird carried also indicate the presence of genes that produce or control the colour of the feather.

The mistake to avoid in the breeding season is, year after year *not* to continue to pair clear bird to clear bird until you have bred out all the green factor genes. I've said before that it's very necessary for all our birds to carry some of these green-carrying genes. By retaining in our breeding stock some *controlled* genes that continue to carry the green factor, we are maintaining the ability to reproduce depth of colour. If we go back some six hundred years or so to the original wild canaries in their native islands they were, and still are, a smoky black colour.

No canary can carry genes for reproducing a green-coloured feather. What the human eye sees as green is a black-brownish feather superimposed onto a yellow background. This is known in the fancy as a yellow–green bird. A Buff green is where the dark colour has been superimposed onto a buff background – it's the same result as when you mix different-coloured paints together.

By breeding from a *very* lightly-green variegated bird, you are maintaining the skilful blending of colours – toned down until the required shade of colour has been achieved. To maintain this colour we cannot dilute further without a visible loss, which has then to be recovered. If you were to visit the bird rooms of the top-ten Norwich exhibitors, you would find that quite a number of the birds were carrying some amount of green variegation in their feathers. The green I would expect to see would be a sharp green colour – not just a blackish-brown colour: we have already seen that it is the green that is the foundation of good colour, be it a clear yellow or a clear buff bird. I am not trying to tell all new fanciers to commence their breeding activities with greens or heavily-variegated birds until they breed the ultimate Norwich. That might never be – and though never is a long time it could well take a very long time indeed.

A BIRD'S PEDIGREE

The most important thing to know about a bird when obtaining any new stock is its pedigree, i.e. from which birds has it been bred on both sides of its parents for the last two generations. Remember that all Norwich canaries should be close rung, so insist on seeing the bird-room register before parting with your money. If no breeding register is to be seen, then no stock should be obtained from that particular bird room. Never just accept what you are told – check the remarks made with the breeding register. It's possible for a good green to be bred by birds that are only lightly variegated. This occurs when a dominant dark gene is being made recessive, and this is not accomplished in two breeding seasons only. It can and does occur after as many as six or seven generations of breeding seasons and is known in the fancy as a throw back. A green or heavily-variegated bird bred in this way will be outstanding for colour, be it yellow or buff. I have personally bred a three-parts dark-yellow green Border that was never beaten when exhibited, so good was it for yellow and green colouring. The reason the bird had such good depth of colour was that the almost clear-feathered parent birds carried genes for the green factor that I had made recessive. At the time the pair of birds mated, a very dominant gene was released. It was a deliberate use of the green-coloured gene factor, the benefits being most noticeable when we have the right colour at the right time and in the right way.

Of course, a lightly-variegated or a ticked bird can produce a similar colour result providing it carries the required rich colour in its system. It must also be paired up to a bird bred from clear parents and not to descendants of greens from the previous year. We must not overlook the fact that a ticked bird, or even a clear bird, is not far removed from a green. It is very well related to pair with a bird closely related to one of green descent, which might be lacking a little for colour but be outstandingly good for type. The breeder can expect that a fair proportion of the young will show both type and colour – making up to birds of show standard.

It's necessary that every breeder knows the pedigree or background of all the breeding stock in his bird room before the start of the breeding season. He is then in a position to look inside his stock as though they were made of clear glass. It is this kind of dedicated breeder who will be next year's breeder of champion Norwich. Once a breeder has acquired two or three years of breeding experience, he can go out to purchase two or three pairs of birds from a successful exhibitor – bearing in mind all that I have said earlier.

RISKS OF FRESH BLOOD

A fancier who wishes to continue to breed from his own stock can do so, but he has to accept the results whatever they may be. I have explained the problems that can occur when fresh blood is brought into the breeding room, for any reason at all, for the first time. Don't purchase an odd bird off the staging direct from a show. I appreciate that in so doing on the surface you will have appeared to have resolved your breeding problem. I personally did this very thing forty years ago, only to find that at the end of the next breeding season the imported young cock had not bred a single bird up to the standard of my own young birds.

APPEARANCE

I have been discussing the various problems associated with Norwich canaries, and while on this subject I must include the appearance of the bird, as this is a prominent feature of *all* Norwich canaries. I have mentioned the importance of colour and the quality of the bird's feather. Equally important, this type of canary must have a neatly-proportioned head, moulded in complete harmony with a stoutly-built body – chest, back, and width. The bird's type or appearance accounts for some 25 points out of 100, so we must have a stout John Bull outline, which immediately sets it apart from other types of exhibition canaries. Do not overlook a small, neat, clear beak; clear, scale-free pink legs and feet; and no excessively long nails.

FORMING YOUR OWN STRAIN

It should be the ultimate goal of all Norwich fanciers to form their own strain or stud of birds that will be prominent competitors in the champion section of any open or national show. This goal is a difficult one to achieve and will require patience, attention to detail, consistency, no undue display of haste or short-cut taking, and, not least, some good luck – whatever form it might take. Today all UK specialist clubs have a set standard of excellence and show classification, so no matter where you live, the rule will always be the same. Remember a good, well-staged bird will always catch a judge's eye.

One of the first things you must acquire is an 'eye' that can readily pick out type in a bird, for no matter how good a bird is for feather quality and colour, if it does not display good Norwich type it will never win its class when in good competition, let alone that award of best Norwich in show. So the first thing you must breed into all your stock is type: if it doesn't have good type, it's not a real Norwich. When you start to breed young Norwich that are good for type, you have put yourself on the ladder to success.

Your next objective should be to breed birds that have a lovely silky finish, with close, even grain in both yellows and buffs. Remember (as is discussed in Chapter 2) when pairing up your birds always pair yellow to buff, as by so doing you will help reduce any feather quality failures. It will not immediately stop you breeding birds that develop lumps or feather cysts, as this is a genetical problem that has to be bred out of your stock. The only sure way to achieve this is never to breed from any bird that has developed or shown any sign of lumps or feather cysts.

To me, the breeding season is the most interesting, busy and reward-ing season of the year. However, if it is to be a successful one, it will have to have been well prepared for months in advance. I start to prepare all my breeding stock in early December by giving them four weeks of winter-time treatment. I give them no artificial form of heating or lighting, and only a plain seed diet of canary and rape seed mixture – no soft food, soaked or sprouted seed – but I do feed a little fresh, frost-free green food twice a week.

In early January I bring spring into the bird room by switching on the heating, which is set to be maintained at a steady 7–10°C (45–50°F), and between ten and twelve hours of daylight. The birds' diet is changed to that corresponding to mid-April in the garden, and the birds then gradually come into a natural breeding condition by the end of March or early April.

You should have completed the selection of all of your proposed breeding stock by mid-November. Should you have previously decided that you want to bring into your breeding room two or three new birds, then these should have been purchased from just one fancier to whom your existing birds are all blood related. Do not buy three or four birds from different breeders, because you will only bring into your bird room birds that are unrelated and that are carrying dominant, adverse genes you are trying to avoid.

If, on giving a last searching look at your breeding stock, you feel that just two of them are of good type, that is fine – these two birds can be the base from which you can commence to build, or breed, your own strain of Norwich. Let us assume that these two birds are a buff cock and a buff hen. Go ahead and pair them up to your best type of yellow hen and yellow cock, and hope to rear two nests of young from each pair, resulting in ten or twelve young birds by mid-July.

Be careful to introduce them to colour food when they are five or six weeks old, and continue using the colour food right through the moult. By October the moult will have been completed. Put all the young birds, which have been bred from the original cock, together in separate show cages and leave them like that for fifteen minutes. Judge each one carefully and critically. If you have bred a young hen that is as good as the adult buff cock for type, and they do not both display the same fault or weakness as each other, then the next breeding season pair up father to daughter. You have now begun to produce your own blood line.

Cage up the young birds you have bred from the adult buff hen. We will assume the birds she has bred are good for type and are all hens, which does not leave a young cock to pair back to the adult hen. Don't worry, the hen has not come to a full stop. At the next breeding season pair her up to the best young cock bred by the adult buff cock. If by the next October the hen has still failed to breed a young cock of good type, then I would consider disposing of this hen, unless she is breeding young hens of excellent type – some birds do this very thing. It is only by breeding from a bird that you find out what her dominant genes are, be they for type, feather, colour, fertility, and so on.

I am firmly convinced that – all things being equal – like will produce like. I do not favour breeding from a big cock and a little hen, I much prefer to breed from birds of equal size. By so doing, the young are more even in size, and in turn your bird room's stock will look, to all visiting fanciers, uniform and line bred. If you have bred a young bird that excels for type, and its nest mates, but the cocks or hens are not of a high standard, don't be too hasty in disposing of them to the first fancier who might be interested in one of them. These close relations can, and do, breed very good young in the next generation.

If all your original purchase of breeding stock was obtained from the same fancier whose birds looked like peas in a pod – nice and even, and had a smooth silky feather – then you should have purchased reliable stock. Just one reminder: check all the birds' closed rings with the breeding register. Young birds bred from this kind of stock can be relied on to be of a high standard; one or two could be very successful on the show bench.

The real factor behind the consistent breeding of show birds is keeping the blood running in family lines. This applies to all types of canary. However, I must stress that this calls for much skill, experience, and patience by the dedicated breeder. Always be aware of both the good points and the bad points of every one of your birds, as these must be counter-balanced when selecting your breeding pairs. All this is not achieved in just one breeding season. The motto is to be slow but sure. It is the final result of years of experience, and of also having the right attitude.

It's not uncommon for a bird to pass on to its young characteristics that are not visible on the surface – features that go back in its ancestry for two or three generations. When selecting breeding stock I always look for type in the hen, that is the shape of the head and body and the wing and tail carriage. For the cock I will be looking for colour, size, and feather. Fifty-one years of experience in breeding canaries has taught me that nine times out of ten it is the cock who has the most control over the outward characteristics of its young. The hen controls or influences the factors for sex, type, and reproductive and feeding abilities, which are the hidden but vitally important features. Like every rule there is, of course, the exception – owing to the characteristics of each pair of birds. Some mark their young with personal features that seem to be fixed in their blood so strongly it is a dominant feature.

There are birds that will pass on certain characteristics not visible in the parents but which go back for two or three generations and indicate the line breeding of the stock birds. Be very careful never to pair up birds that display the same fault or weakness, for an example, two birds that fail in carriage or colour. If you do, you will be breeding into your stock faults you will find difficult to breed out again. Always try to breed into your stock features of excellence. I like to see Norwich, for example, that have nice round cheeks, which help to complete a good head.

If you have to choose a breeding pair from a stud of Norwich with no knowledge of their ancestry, then you should be firmly influenced by the shape and style of the hen's head, in the cock by its depth of colour, feather, and size. As I have mentioned earlier, these are, generally speaking, the features the two sexes are most likely to control.

If you do happen to choose a hen that has good, broad, Norwich head showing at least some clear dark eye, then do not be too easily put off if this is a fault in the cock – as long as he has a good size of a typical Norwich shape, and a good depth of colour. I appreciate that a good-looking pair of Norwich could cost too high a price. If this is the case, look around for a 'balanced' pair of birds, as described earlier.

It must be remembered that, although you have selected or chosen a particular pair of birds, when you breed from them the resultant young can be a disappointment. This is because one or even both of the parent birds carried dominant recessive genes for features you do not desire the young birds to have, less still to display.

You can only prove the value of your breeding stock after you have bred from them. You must also try to ensure that the breeding stock you purchase are unflighted birds. When you pair an unflighted bird to a flighted one (given that the two birds are healthy and vigorous) it will be found that the younger bird's characteristics will be seen more prominently in the birds they breed, but these young birds will be carrying the dominant genes of the older parent bird.

After one or two breeding seasons, a fancier who studies and knows his stock is able to build up and improve the various features of his birds, each year trying to improve a particular weakness – be it for type or feather. Try to breed into your birds a particular good feature – say the head – and then pair up the two birds you have that excel in head quality. In other words, you will be 'doubling up' this good point in most of the young they breed. This is one way the fancier can breed into the birds the desired dominant genes of excellence. Once you have established this feature it is quite easy to continue it in your birds, so much so that other fanciers will be able to tell which are your birds on the show bench – similarly, a fault in a fancier's birds is easily recognised and identified.

The goal to aim for is the breeding of Norwich canaries that carry and show the qualities of a high-class exhibition bird that is outstanding for both type and feature quality. Never sit back and think to yourself that at last you have resolved all your problems – the breeder should at all times be looking for any signs of possible weakness that might have been overlooked.

THE 'DO'S AND 'DON'T'S

(As practised by successful Norwich fanciers)

Some of the essential do's:

1. Only pair a yellow-ground bird to a buff-ground bird.
2. Only breed from those birds that possess the true Norwich type of feather, i.e. those that have the broad, semi-open fan-shape web, and that also readily display their shape and 'quality' of feather.
3. All breeding stock must have good natural colour that enhances the effect or result of colour feeding.
4. Let your Norwich have a natural breeding season by allowing them to have a natural incubation period followed by being given every opportunity to feed and rear their young. But, of course, have a few pairs of feeders such as Rollers, Fifes, or Border pairs, which are paired up at the same time as your Norwich, and which can be used as feeders in an emergency.
5. Always ensure that your Norwich, when feeding young chicks in the nest (especially when the young start to develop feather quills), have a varied and vitamin- and protein-giving diet, to help their feather growth.
6. Always remember that a Norwich canary is one of the – if not *the*

leading 'types' of canary on the show bench. A canary's feather growth requires a large and consistent amount of easily-digested protein food. All Norwich – including young growing chicks in the nest, nest feather young in their first moult, and all adults about to commence their moult – have to be fed a high-protein diet that includes the following: hard-boiled 'fresh' egg, which has been passed through a fine sieve and which ensures that the birds eat an equal amount of both the white albumen as well as the yolk; a small cube of brown bread that has been soaked in a mixture of pasteurised milk and glucose for half an hour, the surplus milk gently removed and the soaked bread sprinkled with maw seed; several times a day, all the feeding hens and moulting birds are to be given a dishful of dried-off 'sprouted' seed – seed that is just commencing to sprout contains four times the amount of vitamins it had as hard dried seed. All the exhibition Norwich's beautiful feather is the result of a very good moult.

7. Do ensure that all your birds enjoy a good, quick moult. Any canary that has a long, drawn-out moult is sure to produce a rough, course feather, which is a severe handicap for an exhibition canary.

8. Do remember to practise what I've discussed about colour feeding: a beautiful colour-fed Norwich is some 85% the result of the fancier's skill in moulting out his birds, be they yellows or buffs.

9. Do maintain a high standard of hygiene in your bird room every day of the year. This also includes personal hygiene on leaving your bird room. This will greatly help to avoid spreading any virus or bacteria – prevention is better than cure.

10. All Norwich *should* – not *must* – be close rung when they are between five and seven days old. Their ring numbers and parentage should be recorded in your bird-room breeding register.

11. A good practice to follow from the earliest stage of the moult is to add to the birds' drinking water once a week a teaspoon of the water resulting from dried saffron flower, which has been allowed to simmer gently in a cupful of boiling water for five minutes. My fifty-one years of canary breeding has taught me that this is Nature's finest way of ensuring a good, clean, quick moult. As Keith Ferry says in *Cage and Aviary Birds*, a quick, clean moult ensures the growth of the finest feather, which is so essential in all show birds. It will also ensure that the colour feeding will result in all the new feathers having an overall evenness of colour.

12. Always remember that a Norwich is best exhibited during its first two show seasons – normally in its third and fourth show seasons it appears to lose its vital appearance of show activity and sparkle. However, much will depend on what kind of a moult it had and its genetic make-up.

13. Do remember that the amount of success you have on the show bench (or lack of it) is often a reflection of a fancier's canary management. This has to be practised daily. You have to be consistent for the whole of the fifty-two weeks of the year.

Here are some of the 'don't's:

1. Always remember that a Norwich is a very large-feathered canary, which has a heavy feather 'under-flue'. This in turn means you must take care to observe the following: when giving your Norwich a bath of water hung on the cage door, ensure that the depth of water inside the bath is less than 12 mm ($\frac{1}{2}$ in) deep; if a Norwich canary has a bath that has a 25-mm (1-in) deep layer of water, the bird's very heavy and thick feathering soaks up the water like blotting paper – it not only takes a long time for the feathers to dry but it also takes a lot out of the Norwich in drop in body temperature, being a strain on the bird's reserve of energy.

2. I have just mentioned that a Norwich has a large and dense feather, when you take into account its flue feathers. It is a canary that has the appearance of having a reserved and quiet nature, very different from that of a Border or New Colour canary. This tends to mask the fact that a Norwich does have a sensitive side, and that it is more easily subjected to the effects of stress. This is particularly true of hens. We hear of fanciers who quite suddenly in the early breeding season finding a hen dead when an early-morning inspection of the bird room is made. I feel that many such cases are the result of stress in the birds, which has inadvertently been introduced by the fancier himself – such as by pairing up their breeding pairs before both birds have reached true breeding condition.

3. It is quite true that a Norwich can be over shown. I was very interested to read in *Cage and Aviary Birds* where Keith Ferry says that his buff Norwich hen, which was awarded 'Supreme Exhibit in Show' at the 1986 National Exhibition of Cage Birds, was only being exhibited for the 'third time that particular season'. I firmly recommend that all Norwich fanciers follow the advice of Keith Ferry and only exhibit their birds once a month. That way they will ensure that the birds will have a three weeks' break between shows, which will ensure that their birds are only shown in their very best condition. In a nut shell, never overshow your birds – this will ensure they are always fresh and free from any 'stress'. The benefit of this will be a good start to the breeding season.

4. Do not be over-anxious to pair up your birds. One bright and sunny late March weekend does not necessarily mean that spring is here and it is time to pair up your birds. If your thoughts are on the pairing up of your Norwich, then you should spend an hour sitting quietly watching both the cocks and the hens. The birds' behaviour will indicate if both sexes have reached true breeding condition.

5. Some Norwich fanciers' birds are subject to lumps or feather cysts. This is a genetic defect and is carried by that particular bird's blood stream. It is thus possible for that bird to pass on this genetic defect to its young. This defect can be dormant in a Norwich, and it may not show any feather defect in that generation. However, it can

re-occur in the next generation. Most thinking fanciers say that the cause of the lumps or feather cysts is the direct result of excessive pairing up of buff to buff for many breeding seasons. There are two points that fully support this theory: Gloster canaries are also subject to feather cysts, and they have also been and are bred buff to buff; on the other hand, the Border canary is completely free of lumps or cysts, and for almost a hundred years they have only been bred yellow paired to buff. Never pass on to an innocent novice Norwich fancier a bird that at some time has had a feather cyst, even if the cyst has been expertly removed and is no longer visible. Always give a novice a square deal when buying his stock birds, because without a steady influx of novices the future for the Norwich is surely in the wrong hands. Eventually it will become extinct just as the London Fancy canary did.

6. Always remember that a Norwich canary – being a large and heavily-feathered canary – often becomes sluggish in its movements. It is in these cases that good condition is often much more difficult to achieve than it is in the much more active breeds such as Borders and New Colours. That is the reason for my saying earlier that you, the fancier, must be consistent in your daily management of your Norwich.

7. Always remember that what I've mentioned in note 6 can often be the cause of a hen failing to feed and rear the young chick she has hatched out. It can also be the reason for a pair of birds producing clear eggs, and this is often the fault of both the cock and the hen. Good fertility is genetically a very important feature, and you have to breed it into your stock, both hens and cocks.

8. Do not pair up your birds just because the calendar says it is now the first day of spring. You must let the breeding condition of your pair of birds tell you when it is time to do this. Do not have a fixed date in your mind – you will find that it will vary one year to the next, much depending on the weather in February, March, and early April.

1981 model of excellence Norwich

A Norwich fault: narrow, mean, and flat above the beak. Note the very coarse buff feather

2
What Makes a Good Norwich?

A first-class exhibition Norwich must have all the following relevant features.

SIZE

The ideal size should be 152–160 mm (6–6½ in) from the tip of its beak to the end of its tail. The bird is of a compact build, the shortest and best comparison being that of a Siberian bullfinch. The bird should be plump and chubby as opposed to long like most other canaries. It must have a bold carriage and be positive in its movements as well as in its position – standing at an angle of about 45 degrees to the perch. The whole bird must be in proportion in accordance with its well-earned description as being the 'John Bull' of the canary fancy.

THE HEAD

The head should be broad across the skull, not round like a Border. However, it should have a nice rise or lift from the base of its beak, going up and over the crown of its head to fall away gradually at the back of the poll or head into the neck in an even curve, with a good expanse throughout. A Norwich that has a small, narrow head should be avoided. For the bird to have a good head when viewed from its beak, it must have width between the eyes. It must also have a fullness of feather between the eyes as the head rises up from the beak – it must not have a narrow, mean appearance. You should also find that the richest colour is also to be found on the crown – the larger the surface, the better the effect. The head is most important. It should display no coarseness but be neat and elegant. Delicate, close feathering should be its characteristic. Coarse feathering, and heavy, over-hanging eyebrows, are to be avoided. The eye should be dark, full, and bright, sparkling with good health. The beak should be neat, finely finished, and free from any appearance of coarseness. It should also be a clear, pinkish-white, free of any discoloration, though the whole or just the upper mandible is sometimes dark. This is not a disqualification, but all other features being equal, the judge will give preference to a clear beak (I am now discussing the classes for 'clear' birds, which do not have any variegated feathers). The discoloured mandible is an indication the bird carries dark genes in its make-up, and if bred from, it could produce young with variegation in their plumage.

THE NECK

The neck must be short and full, the upper part forming, in profile, a perfect line of beauty with the breast.

THE BODY

The breast should be broad, full, and deep and the feather should be very smooth and even in its appearance. Any departure from this spoils the outline of the bird, and is thus a fault. The back should be broad, rising very slightly where it joins the neck to a very gradual curve. The feathers must be compact, showing no inclination to open in the centre. This is not an uncommon feature in some varieties, and is a fault to be avoided. The feathers between the shoulders should be slightly convex, moulding into the neck and back. When you look down on its body, you should see an outline that consists of a series of gentle curves of singular beauty. This is a feature of many canaries today – no hard line is visible in the outline of the bird.

THE WINGS

The wings should not be long but be in proportion to the length of the bird's chubbily-built body outline. They must be carried firmly closed, with no sign of them drooping, and close to the body. The flights from both wings should match feather for feather those on the back, the primaries meeting in a point over the root of the tail without overlapping each other. The closer the flights are packed, the better the colour will be – only the outer edge of each feather is tinged with colour, and so the closer the feathers are carried, the more noticeable the colour will be.

BODY FEATHERS

The shoulders should be well covered, the feathers displaying no projection of any kind. The feathering throughout this part of the body – being very close, compact, and neat – is the most important with show or exhibition birds. It should display a good depth of colour. The body feathers should be compact, not open and coarse, giving the bird a mop-like appearance, for this canary is also a bird of type and quality. The chest must have the appearance of being deep, broad, and full, one of the reasons the bird has acquired the reputation for it being the 'John Bull' of the canary fancy. It is the presence or absence of any coarseness in body feather, or want of general compactness, that indicates the possession (or lack) of 'quality and substance' – a term applied to individual parts of the bird or to a balance of good properties when the bird is taken as a whole.

THE TAIL

The tail's length must be in proportion to the body and wings, being inclined to shortness and to being lightly compact. This helps to display the colour in the tail. The tail feathers must be narrow at the base or root, increasing slightly in width only in the direction of their length. The outer ones should be the largest, with each of the six on either side gradually decreasing in length. This will, of itself, determine the shape and the balance of the bird. I like the tail to be in the shape of a closed fan, narrow at the junction of the body and very slightly radiating out. The feathers should form a V-shaped indentation at the end of the tail. As I've previously stated, the tail feathers so formed emphasise the shape, colour and effective overall balance and colour of the bird. The tail and wing carriage are most important, as is the closed-fan appearance. Neatly folded together it shows off the overall colour in the tail, but when it is partially spread out it completely spoils the effect. Although only five points maximum are allowed for this in the standard of excellence, the overall visual effect is far better when it is closed.

THE LEGS

The only remaining part of the bird which is covered in feathers is the top of the legs or thighs. These should be well covered with fine, silky, flue feathers, right down to the joint or hock. This flue feather must be short, close and compact, with no appearance of trousers. The legs themselves must be set well back at an angle to the body, and their length must be in proportion to the rest of the bird's appearance. They should be inclined to shortness rather than length, for if the legs are too long, the bird appears to be too high above the perch. On the other hand, they must not be too short as this will give the bird the appearance of being very squatty as it stands on its perch. The leg's length should be sufficient to give the bird full control of its body when in a show cage – the legs and feet appearing muscular, taking a firm grip of the perch. They must be free from scales or defects of any kind, including those of the toes and nails, which must not be misformed. All clear birds must have unblemished, clear, pinky-coloured legs and toes.

FEATHER QUALITY

With such a large canary, feather quality is most important if the bird is going to win its class against strong competition. The breeder must, therefore, pay particular attention to this when selecting his breeding pairs. Do not breed from a bird that has a coarse, open-feather web: this is a feather defect to be avoided. When pairing up your birds, always make it a practice to pair a yellow to a buff.

GENERAL APPEARANCE

A Norwich must have the appearance of being a good-natured, relaxed, graceful bird. Although it is one of the larger canaries, it is held in high regard as being an outstanding canary for its type, quality, and colour, which are normally very hard to find in such large types of canary. It is, however, not just size alone that makes for a winner. While size is a feature of almost every variety, it has to give way to other essential features. Where these features are prominent, they are the ones that count the most when selecting breeding stock – irrespective of whatever other minor properties are absent. Size alone is not an overriding factor when other features of the variety are prominent. Size must not, however, be lost sight of, especially in the breeding room. Though it is quite true to say that the best Norwich are invariably of a medium size, and it does appear there is a maximum in mere size alone, the bird must also contain all the other essential features of an exhibition bird. Some breeders have gone for size as their number-one objective in their breeding pairs, but the results have only been partially successful. They have desisted in doing so only when they have found that their young birds – after completing their nest-feather moult – have that extra size but are clearly lacking in the more valuable points such as type, feather quality, colour and general appearance. If all points are equal in two birds, then, of course, the larger bird will win, but in aiming for size as the prime objective, the chances of the other features of the variety being unequal are greatly increased. This approach to breeding pairs does not amount to an admittance that size, as a feature, has been lost not to be regained; rather, it goes to prove that going to the extreme in the development of feather quality and colour has brought about a loss of very coarse webbed feather. In so doing, some loss of size could well have occurred. During the last two decades the breeding of exhibition Norwich canaries by very skilled and knowledgeable breeders and geneticists has resulted in the very high standards of perfection of our leading exhibition birds today – it's a long time ago since 1890 when a meeting took place at the Crystal Palace attended by the then leading exhibitors with a view to improving the appearance of the Norwich.

To repeat what I have said previously about size, size is really important when taken into account with the other essential features of the variety, as size helps to give that noble and commanding appearance that is displayed by a truly outstanding exhibition bird.

COLOUR

Colour is another very important feature in a quality bird and, in conjunction with feather quality, is very noticeable to an experienced breeder's eye. In the standard of excellence's scale, colour can attain ten points. Although colour alone must not be allowed to overrule other features, it is, at the same time, a very important feature in a Norwich, and it is yet another aspect greatly under the control of the individual fancier. The 'ultimate' in colour in all clear birds is seen in both yellows and buffs, and regarded by many fanciers as portraying the ideal Norwich. However, there are many different shades of colour to be seen, varying from a lemonish yellow to a very deep shade of Seville orange. The desired colour, I feel, is a shade approaching that of the Seville orange. I think this is a more realistic comparison than describing it as being between a dark African marigold colour and the pale, lemon colour of the same flower.

I have tried to describe the bird's shape, feather, and colour as having both depth and purity. All varieties of canary are divided into two distinct colour classes – yellows and buffs – which in turn are synonymous with the less well-known terms of 'jonque' and 'mealy'. Although these terms do not represent their real colour, they are regarded as being purely technical. For example, fanciers speak of a bird being a yellow–green or a buff–green, a yellow–cinnamon or a buff–cinnamon (similarly with white-ground coloured canaries) when it is clear that neither of these colours can in reality be yellow or buff. The answer to this is quite simple. Whatever the body colour of a particular canary – whether it is actually yellow, green, cinnamon, or white, whether it be a Lizard canary or a self-coloured canary hybrid – it has two different forms of colour that manifest themselves. One of the colours is much lighter, being the more attractive; the other is dull and flat coloured.

The first colour is described as the yellow form and the other as a buff form. One or other of these two colours is present in *every* canary or canary hybrid. Fifty or sixty years ago the Norwich canary was spoken of in terms of being a jonque or mealy colour. The word 'jonque' is originally French, signifying a jonquil colour, which is self-explanatory. The word 'mealy' only indicates a pale shade of colour, and neither of these two terms are used widely today when referring to Norwich canaries. The accepted terms now are yellow and buff, being common to all types of posture or type canaries.

I have mentioned previously that the accepted ideal Norwich is either a clear yellow or a clear buff bird. However, we often say that the original colour of a canary is green, and that is perfectly true if we go back far enough in history. The original colour of all canaries was a rich, bronzy shade when living in the wild in its native Canary Isles in the North Atlantic Ocean. It was only by very selective breeding over some hundreds of years by canary breeders in different European countries that the clear canary so popular on today's show bench was evolved. This is so much the case that many of today's self-green and self-cinnamon types of posture exhibition birds often carry a lighter shade of dark colour round their vents and throats, although the rest of the bird is rich in colour pigment. Today our canaries vary in colour from that of a young, vivid-green holly leaf, a beautiful shade of cinnamon, a deep, attractive yellow or a clean, fresh buff, and finally to that of pure-white. In self-green or cinnamon Norwich canaries the shade of colour varies, as this is now a colour-fed canary, the green being of a bronzy shade.

A TICKED BIRD

A very attractive canary is one that has a single dark mark on its otherwise completely clear body. This mark is no bigger than a one-pence coin. If we adhere to the true meaning of the word 'tick', this small mark becomes a distinguishing characteristic feature of a particular bird, and it could well be a feature of a particular fancier's line-bred birds. A ticked bird can also be one that has three dark feathers side by side in one wing only or in its tail. The extent of a tick mark on the surface of the feathers can, at the same time, be unlimited as a fine feathering, as long as it does not show on the surface. A dark thigh in one leg only counts as a tick. A ticked bird, however, must carry only one such mark – be it on the body, head, wing, or tail. The feathers that make up the tick may be an entirely dark or grizzle colour, and can be even smaller in size than the one-pence coin. A bird that carries such a mark may, in addition, have a dark under flue – as long as the dark under flue does not show when the bird is standing *undisturbed* on the perch.

THE INFLUENCE OF GREEN GENES IN THE BLOOD

The factor that can have a great effect on the colour of a bird is if its genes carry green or cinnamon. The green factor is the strongest as regards colour, and has the most noticeable effect. Experienced breeders will acknowledge this and make good use of it when selecting their breeding pairs – from it comes fresh vigour and improvement in colour. However, if it's your objective to breed only clear birds, then care must be taken when using breeding stock that carries the green-gene factor. It should, at the same time, be appreciated that a clear bird can carry green-factor genes – it all depends on the particular bird's breeding. Young birds, the first generation removed from green, tend to have the greatest depth of colour, be they yellows or buffs, when their feathers are clear. It's always advisable, therefore, that some of your breeding stock carries green-factor genes. By breeding from these birds you will maintain depth of colour in your clear birds. Always remember that all depth in colour is from dark to light, and that a bird you have bred this way will be the true test. If you were to continue the diluting process by breeding generations of birds from clears only, you would see the resulting loss of colour in the last generations of the young birds.

There is not a great deal of difference between a ticked bird and a variegated one in green-carrying genes. The point is that they both carry the green factor. This variegation in a stud will very often follow a set pattern or common markings, be it on the head, body, wings, or tail, and is a good guide that a particular fancier is line breeding with his birds. If you are thinking of bringing some fresh blood or new stock into your bird room, this is the kind of fancier from whom to purchase your required stock.

To me, the ideal exhibition Norwich is a clear bird, clear in all its feathers, its beak, legs, feet and nails. Like should produce like in all pedigree-bred line stock. It can take a dedicated and skilled breeder many years to reach and maintain this goal, and, therefore, all his surplus stock must command and receive a fair asking price. In all the different types of posture canaries, over a period of two or three decades, each type or variety produces fanciers who have evolved strains of outstanding exhibition canaries. It should be the ultimate aim of all other fanciers to emulate their achievements. This is not an easy task even under the most favourable conditions.

I have read in an old book (written entirely about canaries) that in the 1880s it was quite common to have a class of twenty or more Norwich – and sometimes even more – so that even before the formation of the Norwich Plainhead Club (NPC) the Norwich canary was well established on the show bench. However, even in the early 1900s, the idea of a very lightly-variegated or an evenly-marked bird was usually consigned to the 'Any Other Variety Class'. This may well be the cause for the delay in the development of today's ticked and clear birds, and why today we seldom see an outstanding evenly-marked bird that has both eyes marked as well as the feathers in each wing.

The clear bird must not display a single coloured feather, nor must any of the underflue of the completely-clear body feathers show any trace of dark colour. The competition and high standard of judging at today's major shows means that any coloured under flue visible would be noted quickly to the disadvantage of that particular exhibit. The most likely place any dark under flue would show is on the soft, downy-like cover of the thighs, which would indicate that that particular bird still carried genes for the green factor – even though only a very small amount. The question of what a clear bird is, is generally answered by the definition, 'one that shows no green or variegation', but that is only my opinion. A dark under flue mark does indicate that the bird still carries a little green blood. The extent to which it does will show in the young after the next breeding season. If a bird shows no green at all, then it can be exhibited only in the class for clear birds.

DIFFERENCE BETWEEN YELLOW AND BUFF

I think it is sufficient to say that a yellow bird is one that displays feather of a pure, bright shade, which, after being colour fed before and throughout the moult, has feathers the surface colour of which is a lovely ripe Seville orange. The buff bird is of a similar shade or hue, but does not have the same depth of colour nor the beautiful glistening feather surface. Instead, the surface colour appears to be slightly mealy, and although it still has a ruddy orange shade of colour, it has a veil-like hoar-frosting covering. This colour is softer in places due to the veil-like frosting, but any movement by the bird brings out the freshness of the colour.

Being 'mealy' describes the appearance of the outer edges of the feather, the feathering on the buff being much more dense than that on yellow birds. The under flue is in particular more thick and dense, something that is very noticeable when hand washing a bird. This dense feathering gives a buff bird a big and stout appearance, often seeming to be the larger of the two colours.

STANDARD OF EXCELLENCE

COLOUR: bright, rich, pure and level throughout
SHAPE (head):   round, full and neat
(neck):   short and thick
(body):   short and cobby, with a wide back, well filled in
(chest):   deep, broad, and full
FEATHER: soft and silky, with brilliance and compactness
WINGS AND TAIL: short, compact, with good carriage
SIZE: well proportioned
BEAK: short and stout, and clear
LEGS: well set back
FEET: perfect
CONDITION: healthy, clean, and sound in feather. Streaked bird and marked legs not to disqualify but to count against a bird to some extent.

SCALE OF POINTS FOR JUDGING

TYPE: 25
HEAD: 10
NECK: 10
WINGS: 10
TAIL: 5
LEGS AND FEET: 5
CONDITION: 10
QUALITY OF FEATHER: 10
COLOUR: 10
STAGING: 5
Total: 100

OPEN SHOWS

Schedule of classes

CHAMPION NORWICH CLASSES
1.   Yellow cock, clear or ticked
2.   Yellow hen, clear or ticked
3.   Buff cock, clear or ticked
4.   Buff hen, clear or ticked
5.   Yellow cock, marked, var., or self
6.   Yellow hen, marked, var., or self

7. Buff cock, marked, var., or self
8. Buff hen, marked, var., or self
9. Unflighted yellow cock, clear or ticked
10. Unflighted yellow hen, clear or ticked
11. Unflighted yellow cock, clear or ticked
12. Unflighted buff hen, clear or ticked
13. Unflighted yellow cock, marked, var., or self
14. Unflighted yellow hen, marked, var., or self
15. Unflighted buff cock, marked, var., or self
16. Unflighted buff hen, marked, var., or self
17. Cinnamon yellow cock, self or foul
18. Cinnamon yellowish hen, self or foul
19. Cinnamon buff cock, self or foul
20. Cinnamon buff hen, self or foul
21. White, blue, or fawn, var. or self, cock or hen

NOVICE NORWICH CLASSES
22. Yellow cock, any variety
23. Yellow hen, any variety
24. Buff cock, any variety
25. Buff hen, any variety
26. Unflighted yellow cock, any variety
27. Unflighted yellow hen, any variety
28. Unflighted buff cock, any variety
29. Unflighted buff hen, any variety
30. Cinnamon, yellow, or buff, self or foul, cock or hen

3
The Breeding Room

Of all the aspects of canary breeding, just where you are to keep your birds is perhaps your first consideration. There are a number of alternatives – some of my canary friends use a spare bedroom, others a converted greenhouse, some a wooden shed in the garden, while others use an outdoor brick-built bird room.

PLANNING THE IDEAL ROOM

When I first started to breed Border canaries in May 1935 I had just sold my motor-cycle, so I put my two pairs of birds in the same 2.1 m × 1.5 m (7 ft × 5 ft) wooden shed where I had previously kept it. This shed had an apex-type roof, with a 0.9 m × 0.6 m (3 ft × 2 ft) window in the wall, which faced north. There was no other means of natural daylight.

After my first year with the birds I realised that the inside of the shed (or rather 'canary breeding room') was too dark and in summer too hot. I then put in the east-facing roof, a 0.6 m × 0.6 m (2 ft × 2 ft) window, making quite sure that the roofing felt was water tight. I also made the existing window to open, and I added a 13-mm ($\frac{1}{2}$-in) wire-netting inner door, making it possible to leave the outer door open in the summer. What a great improvement these were to make the following breeding season.

For the last twenty-three years, having moved to a new house, my birds have been kept in a brick-built room that has a 3.4-m (11-ft) tall apex-type roof, to which I have fitted 25-mm (1-in) thick insulation tiles. The 2.5 m (8 ft) north-facing big window I double-glazed with wire-netting inserted into the Georgian-type glass. In the wall facing west is the door with an inner door, with 13-mm ($\frac{1}{2}$-in) wire-netting and a further window. This type of bird room is definitely much cooler in a hot summer, but in the winter months the temperature is colder and the air very humid.

In spite of the fact that for the whole of the winter it is heated by a thermostatically-controlled convector-type electric heater, my birds have been a month later each spring in coming into full breeding condition. From my personal experience, the ideal type of bird room is one constructed of wood, with the windows facing east.

My breeding cages measure 43 cm (17 in) wide, 35 cm (14 in) high, and

A Norwich breeding room with windows facing east

26 cm ($10\frac{1}{2}$ in) deep. They are constructed in threes, with removable partitions, so that in the winter they can be used as flight cages. Each cage front is so constructed that it can be removed by just one finger for cleaning out and repainting purposes. The treble breeding cages are five rows deep, the whole unit being mounted on six castors, thus allowing it to be removed easily when I wish to emulsion paint the brick wall behind it.

Of all the matters that relate to keeping canaries, ensuring that they are kept under healthy conditions is without doubt of prime importance. As they can be regarded as a domesticated bird, their general well-being and the correct environment for them to breed in will depend entirely upon you. It is suggested that once you have decided to breed canaries, the very first thing to do is to visit as many experienced breeders as you can to have a careful look at how their bird rooms are set up and to ask all the questions you can think of.

There are several equally-important things to consider: the hygiene and cleanliness of the stock cages, the equipment (such as the drinkers) as well as that of the bird room itself; all the birds must have plenty of fresh air; no canaries like to be kept where there is a constant draught; the birds, you will find, follow the practice of 'early to bed, early to rise' – the reason I advocate that every bird room should have a window in the east-facing wall, so that your bird room and all its inmates receive the benefits of the early morning sunshine. The first streak of daylight will see your birds on the move, and long before the close of day their heads will be tucked in their wings. We should remember that their day is not the same as ours.

The value of that early morning sunshine to the bird is incalculable –

it enables them to begin work at a time that is in accordance with *their* natural instincts, not least the important task of feeding their young in the nest long before we are even awake.

Canaries will have a longer breeding season when their bird room is kept cool in the summer, and neither they nor their young suffer from the effects of heat exhaustion. If they are affected by excessive heat conditions in the bird room, the result will be a shorter breeding season and an early start to the moult. A cool bird room positively assists the breeding season and can enable you to take a third round if you so wish. A very hot, dry, bird room can often be the cause of your only breeding one round. The question of heat in the bird room (and also *lack* of heat in February and March) has a very pronounced effect on your degree of success when breeding canaries.

If you do have that desirable wooden bird room, you must insulate the walls and roof with 25-mm (1-in) thick PVC, and cover it with hardboard that should be painted with white emulsion paint. This helps to improve the inside illumination level.

It may at first seem strange, but the inside temperature of a non-insulated wooden bird room will actually vary a great deal more over the period of a year than does the outside garden temperature. Every bird has an inbuilt thermostat with which to keep its body temperature fairly constant. It opens and closes its feathers, trapping the air inside the feathers and using it as an insulator. Nature looks after itself in this way – mid-December to mid-January can actually harden and condition a canary. From mid-January onwards, artificial heating should be used and the birds' daily diet increased in both food and vitamin content.

I have already mentioned insulating your bird room with PVC, but do not also forget to double-glaze all the windows. This is a job you can easily and cheaply do for yourself. First obtain sufficient 9-mm ($\frac{3}{8}$-in) square lengths of wood to tack inside the window frames, sealing it all around the outer edges with normal wood-type putty. This will be the most effective when there is a frost – your new inside piece of glass will be free of any moisture. It is also an added security protection against unwanted break-ins, with the associated possible loss of valuable birds.

The handyman will be able to make all the equipment needed for the stock cages – seed hoppers, and support hooks and rings for the glass drinkers. For the seed you will require a dust- and mouse-free type of container. My own is a white-plastic round container sold by Boots for home-made beer brewing.

FIRST AID

I always keep a first-aid air-tight box in my bird room, which contains the following:

1. A small bottle of clear iodine to help stop any bleeding and that will not stain the feathers or skin.
2. A small amount of terramycin – a general antibiotic that, when put in the drinking water, is a very good stimulant for 'soft' birds.

3. A small bottle of whisky – you put 50 per cent water to whisky and gently put it down the back of the bird's throat, should you have a bird that looks soft in condition and does not eat.

4. A small bottle of Abidec, a few drops of which can be added to either the drinking water or a little soft food, if you have a bird that is a little out of condition.

5. A tin of Germolene for any abrasion to the skin of either the legs or feet.

6. A tube of Brolene eye ointment, for any bird that has an infected eye. It should first, with the aid of a little cotton wool, be cleansed gently with a solution of boracic powder and water. It is then wiped dry with a clean piece of cotton wool and, with the little finger, the Brolene eye ointment *very gently* put in.

7. Epsom salts are essential in the breeding season, when the young ones in the nest are between five and nine days old, and the hen is busy removing their frequent voids from the edge of the nest. At this time I put half a teaspoonful in the drinking water and stir it well. It is very useful in keeping the hen's internal system in a normal healthy state, free of any adverse effects from the voids. Canaries can, at any month of the year, be affected by a small stomach virus, which a few days on Epsom salts will rectify.

8. I always keep a bottle of liver-extract tablets to hand, should any of the stock lose their natural vitality at any time. I crush them into powder, one or two liver tablets according to how many birds are affected, and mix it well into their soft food with the aid of a fork. I feed it to the affected birds daily. Two weeks of this diet should see a marked improvement in their condition.

9. No fancier should be without a box of Orovite 7 sachets, which can be obtained from chemists. They are multi-vitamin granules especially suitable for canaries, the granules being dissolved in the drinking water. If given twice a week to all your birds from January to April it will greatly reduce the number of clear eggs and those dead in shell. It cannot be given in too strong a mixture, as the bird's digestive system will only absorb what its body requires. All those vitamins not required will be passed out in its droppings. Use one sachet of powder to two pints of cold water. As we are mainly discussing the breeding room, I will also include young canaries from the age of four weeks, until the completion of their nest-feather moult. These will also benefit from a once-a-week supply of Orovite 7 for during this period they are growing bodily as well as in new feathers, and there must be no interruption to their rate of growth.

10. Keatings powder is an invaluable aid. Those fanciers who feed chickweek to the feeding pairs must have had their nests of young birds covered with northern mite, which will eat and live off the young chicks. If you put Keatings powder inside the nest the hen will continue her feeding without any interruption, and in less than twenty-four hours all the mites will have died.

11. Dried saffron flower is something that does not have any substitute. During the moulting season, should one of the birds commence to moult and then stop moulting, there is one certain cure. Take dried stems of saffron flower, put them in a pan and cover them with water. Simmer them gently for twenty minutes, leave the water to cool, and drain off the now yellow-coloured water. Give this to your birds for four days. Additionally, hang a very damp hessian sack over those cages where the birds are severely affected. Saffron flower is the dried centre stem of a crocus flower. They can be obtained from any herbalist or chemist.

FRESH AIR AND HYGIENE

In planning your bird room be quite sure you have made provision for it to have an adequate supply of fresh air at all times, both during the day and at night time. Canaries thrive on fresh air – their condition is quickly and adversely affected by stale or foul air. At the same time, it should be readily appreciated that all canaries are adversely affected by being exposed to a draught. Your canary room should have two adjustable ventilators with draught deflector plates that can easily be completely closed in cold, windy weather.

One further, extremely important, thing to build into your bird room is a high standard of hygiene at all times. If you practise the following habits you will avoid being plagued by such things as lice, mites (of all kinds), many canary illnesses such as hepatitis, respiratory complaints, enteritis, thrush, loss of feathers (due either to lice or a lack of condition), going light, fungal diseases, and stress. It all depends on a high standard of bird-room hygiene every day of the year, with no attitude of 'I'll leave this or that until next week'. By that time many forms of bacteria could have begun to develop, the result being many varied and adverse effects on any number of your birds.

The following must be done day to day. Remove the previous day's water and wipe and dry the drinker, including the cage front where the drinker has been. Remove all old seed-husks. All forms of green food should be thoroughly washed in a mixture of water and Vanodine V18 and dried before being given to the birds. A weekly must includes the cleaning out of all stock cages, including washing the whole of the inside of the cage with hot water and disinfectant. I always use Dettol, then wipe off the surplus water before replacing the sawdust or shavings, or whatever you use to cover the floor of the cages. The cage perch-ends are dipped in paraffin to discourage any form of mite or lice from using them as a hiding place.

In January, in preparation for the coming breeding season, I paint the inside of my earthenware nest pans with a mixture of Duromytex and water, leaving them exposed to the air to dry off. All the felt nest linings are sterilised by putting them in an old saucepan in a hot oven for about seven minutes. If you start the breeding season with clean birds, cages, breeding equipment, and nesting material, your young birds in the nest will be free from mites and lice, as canaries cannot sweat and thus create lice. We hear from time to time of a breeder's nests being infected by red mite. This must be attributed to a lack of care on the part of the fancier and not the fault of the canaries. The bird-room floor, too, must be washed weekly with hot, soapy water and disinfectant.

Last but by no means the least, you must practise personal hygiene. Every time you come into the house from your bird room, be sure to wash your hands, and in warm weather your face as well. I well remember on one of my many visits to canary fanciers in Australia how a lady fancier told me that during their hot-weather breeding season she developed a rash on her neck. When she showed the rash to her doctor, he asked her if she kept birds. She said that she did – two hundred canaries. The doctor explained that the rash had been caused by bird-room dust in the air coming into contact with the moist skin of her neck – so watch your personal hygiene!

In preparing for the start of the breeding season, all the cages, housing, and breeding cages, both inside and out, should be thoroughly cleaned. The bottoms of the cages need to be well covered with clean, dry sand or sawdust, but I have seen young canaries bred very successfully in cages where the bottoms have been covered with old newspapers. If you intend to use sand, you should ensure that it is clean, sharp sand, or a similar type of river sand. I add to the sand or grit egg-shells that have been pot dried out in a hot oven until they are crisp. All kinds of birds are fond of this kind of liming substance – they will spend a great deal of their time picking over every particle of it.

If you are proposing to use sawdust on the floor of your cages, you should use pine-wood sawdust. When I visited the many different Australian canary bird rooms in Brisbane, Queensland, they all used pine-wood sawdust, with its lovely clean smell – being fortunate in having a local pine-wood sawmill. In Adelaide, South Australia, all the fanciers were using sharp sea-sand because there was no local sawmill. I did notice, however, that canary breeders shared an equal breeding success in these two states. During the breeding season, with the increase in temperature inside the bird room, be sure you continue to sieve all your seed hoppers once a week, even though the birds are not eating as much seed. Once more I should like to stress the importance of keeping your stock in top condition at all times of the year – in so doing you are well on the road to ensuring that your stock will remain free from illness, and that you will find that your birds will quite naturally reach breeding condition.

TEMPERATURE AND VENTILATION

While on the subject of preparing for the breeding season, a Norwich fancier friend of mine has built in his garden a completely covered-in aviary, where he has put all his cross-bred feeder cocks and hens. In spite of some fairly cold frosts, all these birds look to be very fit and well, besides having become very tame – in fact, they will actually sit on your hand to eat their green food. He has, however, been careful to make the aviary draught-proof. From the appearance of these birds, they should be ready to commence breeding at about the same time as the Norwich, which have spent the winter in a heated bird room. In the aviary he proposes to have five hens and two cocks to use as fosters. I have mentioned the use of a heated bird room, but this is *not* a must. In recent winters I personally have not used any form of heating in my brick-built bird room.

For any fancier who is planning to try muling, i.e. where a Norwich hen is used solely to pair to a goldfinch or bullfinch cock, etc., I think the most successful results will be obtained when the two birds are kept together in the winter in a double breeding cage in an unheated bird room. The Norwich canary hen should come into breeding condition at the same time as the British cockbird.

It is generally found that where a fancier has a cool summertime bird room, very often he will enjoy a prolonged breeding season. In 1951 I remember visiting a Border fancier, in his late seventies, who lived in a long row of terraced houses right behind Manchester City football ground. His canary room was a converted concrete air-raid shelter in his backyard, the walls being some 45 cm (18 in) thick solid concrete with a flat, reinforced concrete roof. The inside walls and ceiling had been painted white, and the room was lit by a single electric light-bulb. During the hottest midsummer's day the temperature never exceeded 20°C (70°F), and in midwinter his drinkers never froze. His breeding season always went into late August and his birds were always exhibited in tip-top condition.

I hope that, reading of this adapted canary room, no one will receive the impression that to be a successful fancier you have to spend several hundreds of pounds to obtain an elaborate bird room. We should all remember that the conditions under which a pair of canaries are expected to have a successful breeding season are in a cage very often only 38 cm (15 in) wide, about 28 cm (11 in) deep, and, in nine bird rooms out of ten, they will not receive any direct sunshine. They have to make the best of the position of the cage, as they are unable to preen their feathers in direct sunshine, while a few will have little or no protection from the rays of the summer sun. In other words, a breeding pair have to make the best of the position of their cage, and they are thus entirely dependent upon the care and forethought of the fancier for their well-being in the form of a balanced diet and fresh, clean water, as required at the different months of the year.

There is no doubt that the question of the bird room's aspect, windows, and general suitability should be one on which we feel perfectly satisfied, as much will depend upon this decision. It will often be the key to the solution of the question of varying degrees of success.

As already mentioned, the question of draughts and ventilation demands careful consideration in connection with any bird room, and I would like to detail some arrangements that will be found useful. Some things will depend on the room itself. For example, some thirty-five years ago I visited a well-known breeder of Yorkshire canaries – F. Agopion – who lived in Didsbury, South Manchester. He kept his birds in an attic that had one protruding window, and a single electric light-bulb. It should be borne in mind that in those days attic windows were well-known for their draughtiness, but this had been taken good care of, and a wire-mesh frame had been fitted to the window in case a bird might be free in the room while the window was open. In those days the now familiar electric-light dimmer had not been invented, but a similar result was obtained by the use of a 25-watt carbon filament bulb, which gave a soft yellow or dim light.

Ventilation in the room consisted of air bricks in the wall, and these were very effective: at no time was there a stale atmosphere. However, because it was an attic bird room it was quite considerably affected by both frost and hot sunshine, but this did not appear to adversely affect the breeding results.

If it is practical for a fancier to install some form of heating controlled by a thermostat in his bird room then, if the thermostat is set for a maximum of between 4°C and 10°C (40°F and 50°F), it is surprising just how much sooner the birds will come into breeding condition in the spring. It is just the same with birds in the wild where, when in January, February and March there is little or no frost, the blackbirds, thrushes, dunnocks and sparrows will all commence their breeding activities a month early.

There is just one more precaution to be taken in the bird room and that is to ensure that it is 100 per cent mice proof. By this I mean make sure there is no possible place where a mouse could gain access to your bird room. The most effective way to ensure this is to nail strips of tin, bent at a right angle, on the floor and sides of the bird room. The ever-sharp teeth of a mouse will eat their way through anything else, and before you have seen one, they will have a nest of young ones. If these are left free for three months then each young female will also have a nest. That old saying 'breeding like mice' has been well earned!

AN AUSTRALIAN BREEDING ROOM

It is always interesting to hear how fanciers in other parts of the world look after their birds, and here is how one nationally-known fancier does for his stock. The most consistently successful breeder and exhibitor of Yorkshire canaries in the whole of Australia at the present time is Stan Nicholes of Melbourne, Victoria, and the following are his remarks for bird-room management for a successful breeding season:

To obtain top breeding results the fancier must start preparations from the beginning of winter, with attention to the following details:

1.   The addition of Ornithon to the drinking water – 1 teaspoon to 1 litre, three days on and one day plain water – also Vetemul, half a teaspoon added to egg-food mixture for each egg used. These

supplements provide all the necessary minerals, etc., to improve fertility and prevent dead in the shell.

2. Winter feeding programme: plain canary seed daily; a bowl of fresh, fine shell-grit; fresh, clean cuttlefish attached to cage. My own winter feeding programme is as follows:

Monday
One or two of the following green foods: broccoli, chicory, Chinese cabbage, young cauliflower leaves, and any available seeded grasses, all thoroughly washed before feeding. Also, approximately one-quarter teaspoon niger seed to each bird.

Tuesday
Egg-food mixture – *to one egg*:

  1 heaped tablespoon commercial soft food mixture
  1 heaped teaspoon Glucodin
  1 heaped tablespoon Farex
  1 level tablespoon blue maw seed
  $\frac{1}{2}$ level teaspoon calcium powder
  $\frac{1}{2}$ teaspoon Vetemul

Wednesday
Mixed seed consisting of half tonic seed and half ground seeds – safflower, sunflower kernels, rape, and hulled oats.

Thursday
Green food, grated or boiled carrot, and half a teaspoon niger seed to each bird.

Friday
Sprouted seed. I consider this the most essential food for conditioning the breeding stock and the most popular and nutritious for the parents to feed their young. (The sprouting procedure is given below.)

Saturday
Same as Monday.

Sunday
Same as Tuesday.

To sprout seeds
I use one cup each of safflower, grey sunflower, white lettuce, plain canary, and Jap millet, and two cups of black rape seed.

In these proportions the seeds are mixed in a large enough quantity to last through the entire breeding season. It is most important to ensure that all the seeds are alive and will sprout. I have found that only rape and lettuce fail and go mouldy, and if fed to the birds in this state they can cause serious illness. As a safeguard, I always test a small quantity of rape and lettuce before buying the full amount required for the breeding season.

I soak one or two large cups of the mixed seeds (depending on the number of birds to be fed) in a bowl of water for twenty-four hours in cold weather, or four to six hours in hot weather – soaking for too

Sprouting seed

long in hot weather can cause the seed to go sour and to fail to sprout. Having experimented with many recognised ways of sprouting seed, I have found the following the most successful.

I use five trays, made with a wood frame and flywire base, which slide into a steel stand with approximately 8 cm (3 in) space between the trays, each of which is covered with towelling. The soaked seed is washed in a strainer under running water and spread evenly over the trays. These are then covered with a further piece of towelling that has been thoroughly wetted. Each tray is given a light spray of water every morning, and even twice a day in very hot weather, as they must be kept moist.

At three to five days the seeds should be ready to feed and at this time I scrape them off the towelling and wash them as before in a strainer under running water. They are then rolled in a tea towel to rid them of excess water and are ready to feed to the birds. When the trays are emptied the towels should be scraped clean, washed, and used again. I personally consider sprouted seeds the most important single factor in any success I have had rearing Yorkshires over the last twenty-five years.

3. Breeding cabinets should be rubbed down with sandpaper and given a coat of enamel to ensure a vermin-free start.

4. Clean and disinfect nest pans and store them ready for use during the busy breeding season.

5. Prepare enough nesting material for the entire breeding season and store it in containers. This saves valuable time for the actual

breeding jobs. I boil hessian bags and, when dry, these are cut into 8 cm (3 in) lengths and teased out to give the finishing touch to the nests.

6. I fly the cocks and hens in separate flights from the end of the show season, about mid-December, until they are put in their breeding cabinets mid-February. The flights are assembled temporarily in the bird room and measure approximately 2.5 m (8 ft) high, 1 m (3 ft 6 in) deep and 1.2 m (4 ft) wide. Perches are placed 15 cm (6 in) from the roof, which allows the birds an upward flight of approximately 2 m (7 ft) and gives them the exercise they need to bring them into top condition for their breeding responsibilities. While in the flights they are provided with a bath three to four times a week.

7. After the show season is a good time to worm out your birds, especially if they have been in an outdoor flight. It is much better to be feeding your birds than the worms, and most pet shops have a recommended syrup with directions for its use.

8. When the birds are transferred from the flights to their breeding cabinets they are each dusted with Mala-Verm dusting powder to free them of vermin. The beak and toenails are also cut and they are trimmed heavily around the vent, leaving the feelers intact. The feet and legs must be clean but, if scaly, one of the ointments available for this problem should be used.

Artificial heating
For the last two years I have used this during the months of February and March and found it excellent. I use an ordinary hot-air blower and a thermostat, which I set at 17°C (62°F), and I feel it is a safeguard against the chilly periods we have early in the breeding season.

Artificial light
I use this right through the breeding season, giving at least one and a half hours of extra light at night for extra feeding time. I use an automatic timer and dimmer, which takes about half an hour to fade out.

The use of feeders as foster parents
I consider it necessary to have three to four pairs of feeders, particularly if you are breeding the larger-type canaries such as Yorkshire, Norwich, and crest breds. I use Red, Lizards, Glosters, and common canaries as these are smaller, more vital, and energetic in their feeding duties. Each year I select the best feeders and raise a few of their young for future use. Although I find that Yorkshire hens in top breeding condition generally prove good mothers, you do strike the odd, big, lazy hen that could let you down.

As an insurance against this I put up two pairs of feeders at the same time as I mate up my very top three or four pairs of Yorkshires, and swap the eggs over. The Yorkshire eggs are marked with a red Y and

I make the necessary note in my breeding records. This can save a heartbreak if a Yorkshire hen fails to feed her young.

All experienced fanciers know how difficult it is to obtain the really top birds. For example, I may put up twenty pairs but only consider five pairs of the class likely to produce champions. Now, by using feeders, I will get four rounds from these top birds instead of three, and thus have the opportunity of achieving a higher standard of youngsters. The procedure used is as follows:

First round My top pair of champion Yorkshires are allowed to bring up their first nest of young, or the feeders' young if the eggs have been swapped.

Second round The eggs are taken away and put under feeders and the hen is allowed to sit for a few days, when the nest is taken out. Within a week she will be nesting again. This has saved three weeks, and she can be allowed to bring up the **third round**.

Fourth round The feeders are again used to bring up this round. This means that the champion Yorkshire hen has laid four rounds of eggs, which would not sap her strength at all, and the heavy feeding responsibilities that *do* take a lot out of a hen have been reduced to only two rounds.

Having feeders available can also reduce the risk if a top hen leaves her eggs, as they can be transferred to the feeders. As an example, I have had a Yorkshire hen who, after sitting on full eggs for ten days, finally left them. I have put the eggs under a feeder who had only been sitting a few days and she has reared them successfully.

A question often asked of me is, 'When do you pair up your Yorkshires?' More or less, I leave the final decision to the hens themselves. Early in March I inspect the hens in the flight and any hen

A Norwich double breeding cage, made by Bill Chilton

whose abdomen is full, round, and pink in colour is ready to be paired up. Others that are not in this condition are left for a couple of weeks then checked again for breeding fitness. When a hen is really ready to commence her breeding activities you can see a yellow line down the centre of the abdomen. On the other hand, only disappointment can result from mating up a hen whose abdomen is flat with the skin wrinkled and leathery.

When the fit hen is placed in the breeding unit, I put the cock bird in with her and if there is fighting I divide the breeding cage with a slide that has 25-mm (1-in) diameter holes approximately 8 cm (3 in) from the floor. This prevents any damage to the hen and usually in a day or two they are friendly – the cock will feed the hen through the holes in the slide. When all appears quiet I remove the slide and leave the birds together. I also put a little nesting material in the wire of the front and when you see the hen consistently carrying this material in her beak you know she is ready. Only then do I put the nest pan in with a sufficient supply of material for her to start building.

This procedure needs patience, but is much better than forcing the birds into breeding before they are really ready. The latter can only result in clear eggs, and so on.

When the hen lays I take the egg away each day and place it in a small drawer, lined on the bottom with sawdust for safety, replacing it in the nest with a dummy egg. While the eggs are in the drawer they should be turned over each day as they would be in the nest. On the fourth day I return the eggs to the nest, removing the dummies. The obvious advantage of this method is that the youngsters all hatch out on the same day. I have often kept a setting of eggs up to eight days because the hen would not sit, turning them each morning as mentioned, before finally placing them under a feeder hen.

When the hen has been sitting for five to six days I check the eggs to see if they are full. This is a simple task, but care is necessary or the egg could be damaged. Hold the egg at each end between thumb and first finger against the sunshine or an electric light. If you cannot see

Canary egg drawer

through the egg it is most likely full. On the other hand, if light can be seen through the egg it is quite possibly clear. I would allow a further three days, and if the eggs are still clear I would take the nest out and mate the hen up again when she starts carrying nesting material.

Eggs are due to hatch on the thirteenth day after being set, but sometimes a hen does not sit as tightly as she should, particularly in the first few days, and the eggs may not hatch until the fourteenth or fifteenth day. On the morning of the thirteenth day I provide a bath and this, as well as being refreshing for the hen, provides essential moisture for the nest and eggs. If the hen does not bathe, I use a fine spray of water over the nest and eggs. Also on the morning of the thirteenth day I carefully place the eggs in a cup, which has been filled with warm water. This should activate the youngster in the egg and it will bob up and down. If the egg does not move the youngster is probably dead in the shell. When this happens I wait until the fifteenth day and repeat the procedure. If there is still no result I take the nest out and once again replace it when I see the hen carrying nesting material.

The day the youngsters are hatched, a close watch must be kept to see that they are not thrown out of the nest by accident. This can happen when the hen throws out a piece of eggshell with a youngster adhered to it. If it does happen I put the young one back under the mother for approximately five minutes to give it time to recover.

4
Feeding and Diet

From ancient times, humanity has developed the habit of keeping all kinds of birds in captivity – because of its sheer fascination with them. Centuries ago in the UK, it was the highlight of the day when the master and his servant took their captive birds of prey out in the countryside, hunting for game birds such as pheasants and partridges. At the same time, across the other side of the world, Chinese fishermen were using cormorants to catch fish.

In the UK, canaries have been kept and bred for over four hundred years, so that breeders have gradually developed what are now called 'type canaries'. Some of the earliest breeds or types (such as the London Fancy and Lancashire Coppy) became extinct in the early part of this century, but I am pleased to say that the Lancashire Coppy, thanks to the efforts of members of the Old Variety Canary Association, is well on the road to being re-evolved to its original standard.

Between 1865 and 1890, the canary breeders laid down very long-lasting rules for what were to become the following breeds of canaries: Borders, Yorkshire, and Norwich canaries. Since that time two further types have become established – the Gloster and Fife. These five completely different types are now being bred and exhibited worldwide in Canada, Australia, the USA, and Europe. During the past forty years almost all the canary specialist societies have made great efforts to update and harmonise their individual standards of excellence. This has produced very beneficial results for the canary fancy, particularly the Border fancy. At the annual show of the British Border Fancy Canary Club, an entry of almost 2,400 Wee Gems has been received, with some unflighted classes having as many as 97 Borders in a single class.

VITAMINS

At the same time, much thought and effort has been put into researching the vitamin requirements of canaries. It has only been over the last thirty years that both canary fanciers and leading suppliers of pet foods have begun to research just what is vital to keep the various varieties of cage birds in tip-top condition. This includes such things as show condition; breeding condition; production of fertile eggs; good hatching performance; and what enables a bird to produce feathers of outstanding show quality. These are all so essential in Norwich canaries.

I would say that the vast majority of present-day fanciers are more conscious of these things than any previous generation of canary breeders. Fifty-five years ago, when I first started to breed Borders, the diet fed to pairs of breeding canaries consisted of hard-boiled eggs cut in half, bread and milk, crushed arrow-wheat biscuit, and chickweed. All this being so, and without a full understanding of feeding a 'vitamin-balanced diet', the fanciers of those years actually bred more young birds per nest than today's average breeder is able to produce!

Looking back over the period 1955 to 1965, I would think these were ten years of consistently good breeding seasons for both the average number of canaries bred per nest, and the quality of feather in the young. It was during these years that a number of the leading Border and Norwich breeders allowed their soaked seed to sprout before giving it to the breeding pairs. It has only been in recent years that scientists in the bird world have told us that sprouted clean seed has four times the vitamin content of ordinary soaked seed. However, I think some of today's food-sales gimmicks are over-exaggerated, tending to blind many fanciers with their scientific terminology.

On the other hand, it's certainly true that feeding vitamins to our birds is very necessary, and most fanciers will readily agree with this. To begin with, we'll look at vitamins – those organic substances that occur in food and that are essential to good health. The following are some of the more essential of them.

Vitamin A The birds have a light-sensitive membrane at the back of the eye, and if a bird is deficient in vitamin A it will be affected by poor sight. Vitamin A is commonly found in eggs, fresh green food, and the yellow flowers of growing rape plants.

Vitamin B Vitamin B1 is a valuable white crystal that helps to control the body cells, and is present in most seeds that are in a good condition, such as canary and rape seeds. The vitamin B group has a wide spectrum, including B2, B3, and B6. These are to be found in fresh green food and Glucodin.

Vitamin C or Ascorbic acid This is also present in fresh green foods and citrus fruit, and is essential for healthy body organs and tissues. Only small quantities are produced within the bird itself. The main function of this vitamin is to feed and maintain the capillaries carrying the blood. It also affects the tenderness of the legs and feet, and helps to control any bleeding.

Vitamin D The main function of this vitamin is to assist the bird's system in absorbing and making use of calcium and phosphates in the workings of the body. It is obtained from the ultra-violet rays of sunlight, and also from eggs, milk, and seeds. A lack of vitamin D can be one of the reasons hens lay soft-shelled eggs, and produce defects in their chicks and young birds.

Vitamin E This is particularly important before and during the breeding season, as one of its main functions is to maintain the condition of body cells – of vital importance during the breeding season. The best sources of vitamin E are the use of sprouted, mixed seed and wheat-germ oil.

The feeding of vitamins to our birds is part of good management, perhaps the most important times being both before and during the breeding season, as well as to young growing birds. For the average non-technically-minded fancier to give his canaries the correct type of vitamins in the amount their systems require, Orovite 7 multi-vitamin granules should be added to the drinking water (see Chapter 3).

A BALANCED DIET

I have, over many years of writing articles in the fancy press, stressed the importance of feeding your birds a properly balanced diet that will enable them to live a fully active life. To the fancier this will, in turn, mean successful breeding seasons, with none or very few clear eggs or dead in shell. The maintenance of good health is entirely dependent on your birds having daily access to suitable nutrition, because it is from the metabolism of nutrient foods that energy is released, which the birds can use to enable them to live full and active lives.

The following are the main nutrients to which a healthy bird must have easy access: clean water, proteins, carbohydrates, mineral salts, and

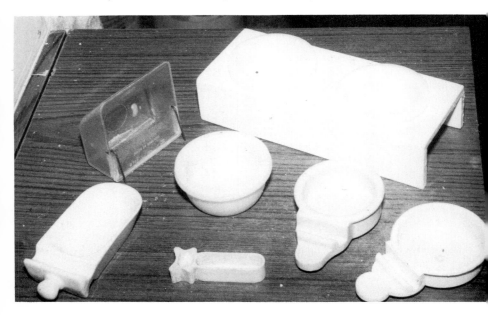

Various feeding dishes

and a full range of vitamins. All these must be readily available in their various forms the full fifty-two weeks of the year. The following list describes how they function.

Clean water Clean water not only satisfies a bird's thirst but is also its main source of nutrient, for it carries with it any multi-vitamins that are not readily available in its normal diet of hard seed. It is also necessary to the chemical reactions involved in such things as the digestion of proteins and carbohydrates. It helps also to replace expended body fluids. A normal, healthy bird will take small but frequent drinks of water – so you will appreciate why I stress that it must be clean and fresh at all times.

Proteins Proteins have to be fed to our canaries in one form or another, as their own systems do not produce them. After being digested they are circulated through the blood stream to cells and tissues. Protein is the main source of feather reproduction. It assists in the production of enzymes, which are living cells that act as catalysts in bio-chemical reactions. Protein is also the source of nitrogen and anti-bodies, which are the birds' main defence against disease and infection. For these reasons I advise the feeding of soft food mixed with hard-boiled egg at least once every week of the year.

Carbohydrates These are substances containing the elements carbon, hydrogen, and oxygen. They all affect a bird's energy and respiration,

Useful feeding equipment: a multi-purpose plastic food or water container and clip-on drinker

and are contained in glucose. Most fanciers put it in their soft food in the form of glucodin obtainable from most chemists. Excess carbohydrates are stored in a bird's body in the form of fat – this is why, with my breeding hens in the winter months, I like to see a pale yellow colour under the skin round their vents. This fat indicates both an adequate reserve of carbohydrates and protection from severe cold. It is also a nutrient for the ovaries, for as the hen comes into breeding condition she does not have to depend entirely on her blood stream for it at that time of year. While a bird's system does produce it from hard seed, experienced fanciers have always added Glucodin to the soft food – especially both before and during the breeding season to maintain maximum energy in the breeding stock.

Cellulose Cellulose provides both roughage and starch, which are essential for health and vigour. They are obtained from good-quality hard seed.

Fats and Oils Birds, like humans, require fats and oils in the right proportion. They are helpful to a bird in absorbing any effect from shock, and they assist the bird in winter to maintain a regular body temperature. One of the main sources of oil is cod-liver oil, which is mixed with the basic seed diet during the winter months.

Steroids Steroids are not produced naturally by the bird. Their main function is to produce cholesterol. You give it to your birds in the form of hard-boiled egg.

Hydrocarbons Hydrocarbons are compounds of hydrogen and carbon. They are required by birds during the winter months to ensure that the birds' high body temperature is maintained. They are not as necessary during the summer. The birds obtain this from such seeds as niger, linseed, and sunflower.

Mineral Salts Mineral salts are as essential to all bird life as they are to human beings. They can be given to our birds in various ways.

SALT For many years I have given salt to my birds in the form of small pieces of cattle rock-salt, which I first soaked for an hour in cold water. Birds love to remove the salty water from the surface of rock-salt, especially during the winter months.

CALCIUM Calcium is especially important to breeding hens during mid-winter and early and late spring, as almost 80 per cent of each egg-shell consists of calcium eaten by the bird. The remaining calcium is obtained from the bird's in-built reserves. Just before a hen is due to lay her first egg, I take a very sharp knife and peel off pieces of cuttlefish bone, just as you would peel an apple, and give this to the hen in a soft food dish. Cuttlefish is almost 100 per cent calcium. It is also needed by young, growing canaries, to assist with the development of both their bodies and bones.

One thing that contains a wide spectrum of different mineral salts is granulated charcoal. Given all the year round (except during the show season, so as to avoid our exhibition birds developing dirty grey faces) it is one of the most practical ways of maintaining high standards of fitness in all our stock.

Vitamins As I have mentioned earlier, these are of vital importance to our birds for their continued good health and vitality. The essential vitamins are A, B1, B2, B3, B6, C, D, and E. It is of vital importance that all these vitamins are included in our birds' daily diet. If we feed a weekly diet that includes all the following food items then the birds will have access to all the required vitamins: green food, such as dandelion, watercress, rape tender leaves, and chickweed; the yellow flowers of growing rape plants; dried yeast; eggs; wheat-germ; well-washed sprouted mixed seeds; cod-liver oil; a little piece of bread soaked in milk and glucose; maw seed; and a little sunflower seed. It must be remembered that the correct way to give these foods to our birds is in small quantities daily. In so doing the bird's digestive system will extract the vitamins so vital to its general good health at all times of the year. To complete your stock's good management, a daily supply of fresh drinking water should be supplied in a clean container.

Watercress

Shepherd's purse

Persicary

Seeding plantain

Green food A small supply of fresh green food should be given every day of the year. Green foods I feed my birds start with chicory, watercress, apple skins, carrot slices, dandelion roots, sprout leaves (not frosted), and then, as they become available, spinach leaves, young growing rape-plant leaves with its yellow flowers, seeding chickweed, seeding heads of chicory, young dandelion leaves, seeding heads of dandelion with its fluff cut off with a pair of scissors, green seeding heads of dock, short seeding heads of grass, shepherd's purse seed, heads of any colour, cinnamonish red seeding heads of plantain, well-washed sprouted mixed seed once a week during mid-winter, increasing their usage from early February onwards. Canaries that are regularly fed such a wide spectrum of green food should be full of vitality all the year round. They should seldom be in need of the assistance of any man-made artificial stimulants.

5
Pairing, Management and Line Breeding

Selecting the right birds to pair together is clearly the difference between breeding a best Norwich, champion or novice, or breeding birds for the local pet shop. I have written about this subject in detail in my book, *Exhibition Canaries*, but the essential point, as I have already stated in Chapter 1, is to know the background of your breeding stock. Always remember that the amount of success (or lack of it) during the breeding season will depend solely on the genes carried in the blood stream of the parent bird.

GENES

Genes, as mentioned in Chapter 1, can be either recessive or dominant. If they are recessive (and thus not visible in the parent) they will appear in the first or second generation of young birds. If a bird's genes are dominant this will mean that a bird's points of excellence should be passed on to its young ones. If a good adult bird does not pass on these points of excellence, you must replace its partner, as this bird's genes are dominant over the other bird's genes. It is only possible to discover these features in your stock by breeding from them.

Most experienced breeders, when they bring into their breeding room some fresh blood in the form of a cock bird, will first test pair it to a hen who the previous breeding season bred young birds that all carried her points of excellence. If, from this test pairing, 50 per cent or more of the young ones are like the cock bird, then you have proved that his genes are dominant and that it is safe to pair him to several of your best hens. From these pairings you will breed good young ones.

You will have also proved that this cock will make an excellent line bird to breed from, and the next breeding season he should be paired up to his best daughter. From this pairing you will breed good birds, all of which will have their father's good features. It is only by breeding from your birds that you will be able to know which carry dominant genes, and which recessive genes. I cannot stress enough that it is next to impossible to start at the bottom and reach the top if the breeder's stock is inferior.

TYPE, SIZE, FEATHER AND COLOUR

It is usually found that the off-spring of medium-sized birds are more even, and their points better balanced, than the off-spring bred from a large cock and a small hen, or from a small cock and a large hen. If you cannot obtain two birds of, say, 16 cm (6 in) each, then the size should be on the cock's side. It should also have a good, deep colour and a good, round, broad, clean head, free from any browiness. The hen should excel in good type and quality of feather. Normally, you will find that type in the young will come from the hen, and that size and colour will generally come from the cock. I always like a canary to 'look' its sex, particularly so when birds are being judged for specials.

When selecting your breeding pairs always pair a yellow ground-coloured bird to a buff-coloured one. In so doing you will achieve two things: feather texture, quality, and an evenness of colour; and a greatly reduced possibility of breeding birds that will develop feather cysts or so-called lumps – such as are found in some Norwich and Gloster canaries. Feather quality in a Norwich is a must if you are going to breed Norwich that excel in type and quality. It is difficult enough to breed birds of really good type, but it is even more so to breed Norwich that are outstanding in their quality of feather. There is nothing more pleasing to the eye than a Norwich that is outstanding for both type and quality of feather (which includes colour, of course), and that has been staged to win.

It is the consistent pairing up of yellow to buff that is the reason – I am sure – why year after year tens of thousands of Norwich are perfect and completely free of any form of lump. So just when, and for what reason, should we deviate from this principle? If your birds are becoming fine feathered but still true to type, and you are unable to obtain a fresh blood line to correct the fault, or if you wish to keep to your own blood line, try double buffing. On no account, however, must either of the pair of birds show any signs of roughness of feather – this undesirable quality is quickly transmitted, and birds that have this appearance have little chance on the show bench when in good competition. By pairing two buffs you will increase the size of your birds, as well as correcting the feather quality. In double-buffing, great care must be exercised or your birds could be too big, and a little coarse in feather.

For those fanciers who breed self-greens and cinnamons, if the dark pencilling on the bird's back and thighs is getting too fine, then by double-buffing you will increase the web of the feather and also the dark pencilling – but be careful when selecting your pairs that you keep feather quality.

When and why do we double-yellow? If you examine a Norwich's feather under a microscope you will find that a yellow-ground feather – compared to a buff feather – has a different shape. A yellow feather is not quite as broad as a buff, but it is a little longer. So, if your birds are a little too broad but short in length, that is the time to try double-yellowing. Some fanciers might ask how this will affect the colour of the young birds. Each colour, be it yellow, buff, white, green or cinnamon, is controlled by a single gene, and the colour produced by a single gene will be just as good as that produced by either a double-yellow or double-buff pairing.

When breeding with a view to producing first-class show birds, it is best to have a definite breeding plan in mind. First, breed only from the best quality stock. On the question of inbreeding there are many points of view, but successful canary breeding is just like breeding race horses – it is all a matter of blood lines and dominant genes. This is explained more fully in my book mentioned above.

The fancier who is constantly introducing hereditary tendencies about which he knows very little, and which turn up in the young unexpectedly, owes this to the adults carrying unwanted dominant genes. It must be remembered that every variety of canary has points that demand patience to acquire. No breeder can expect to make any headway or remain at the top of his fancy if each year he makes a practice of selling his best birds. You cannot have both the money from selling your best birds and, at the same time, retain your essential stock. In my opinion, the birds always come first.

I have already explained that the colour of a canary is controlled solely by a single gene, and with this in mind, if – like me – you breed white-ground birds, you should never hesitate to pair up their young to your normal-coloured birds. I have heard experienced fanciers advise against doing this as it will dilute the colour of any young they may breed. This is genetically untrue. I personally advise all fanciers to keep a few white-ground birds in their bird room because they will in no way adversely affect either feather quality or colour. Breeders are often inclined to adopt different methods in an effort to obtain results when experience tells them not to.

I am also a firm advocate that all Norwich breeders should not be without a self- or three-parts dark-green-coloured bird in their bird room. I do not mean a dark-coloured bird, but one that has a real, green, holly-leaf green: the outside colour would be a yellow and the inside colour a buff green, both of which are truly lovely birds. The use of a green-coloured bird will greatly assist in maintaining the depth of colour of your normal birds. Good results will be obtained if you pair an unflighted hen to a two- or three-year-old green cock, provided, of course, that both birds are healthy and well, and are free from scaly legs or butt flights.

PEDIGREE OR LINE BREEDING

In all forms of highly-bred live stock, the points that characterise a particular animal or bird are the results of years of carefully selecting breeding stock until a required standard of excellence has been attained. This is precisely what has happened in the world of breeding exhibition canaries, for example, the spangles and rowings of a Lizard canary and the black pencilling on the back and the sides of an exhibition green

Norwich canary. The same applies to the lovely cinnamon Norwich canary, which has to carry the very dark brown pencilling on its back and sides.

Such markings may, from time to time, occur as if by accident in an individual bird, but if it occurs repeatedly as a family characteristic, it must have been bred into the birds when the breeding pairs were selected.

The distinctive colour and markings of a bird are due solely to its genetic make-up – and every bird carries genes and chromosomes that control the whole of its appearance. These genes are first introduced when pairs of birds mate, and they multiply and develop within the egg as incubation takes place.

The pedigree of a bird, as we term it today, is based purely on the belief that an individual has the genetic ability to pass its quality on to its young. The actual pedigree is of value in so far as it can only prove that no cross-breeding has taken place in the recent past. As a certificate, a bird's pedigree is not completely reliable. The bird's value can only be proved by breeding it with another bird.

Where pedigree records are kept, only the individuals that closely approach their particular standard of excellence should be considered – with a nest of birds they should be close rung and so identifiable. There is, however, one section of the fancy where this is strictly not done. This is by the majority of UK Border canary breeders, who use celluloid split rings because Border convention ruling is that all rings are optional. In every other country in the world where I have judged Borders (Europe, Australia and the USA) Borders can be exhibited only as long as they are close rung and owner bred. This being the case, we should only concentrate on those kinds that really do comply with the standard of excellence.

Let us suppose you are completely new to canary breeding. You have just bought two pairs of canaries and are about to commence breeding from them with a view to establishing your own strain. The young birds should be carefully moulted out. Having done this, and got them used to their show cage, you should then compare them with their breed's outline drawing and written standard of excellence. Let us presume that two of the young birds do resemble the outline drawing, and have a look of 'type' at least to equal that of their parents. You can keep these two young birds to breed from. To obtain two young birds to pair them to, you should take them to the breeder from whom you obtained your original birds, thus keeping to the same blood line. (By this time you should have also visited a few shows and had a good look at the two birds that were placed first and second in your variety of canary. In so doing you will learn to acquire an eye for type.)

When you go to obtain your new young birds, make quite certain that the birds you purchase do not have the same faults as your existing birds. Try – if it is at all possible – to obtain birds that excel where your existing birds have faults. You can now make your first attempts at forming your own line or stud of birds. We will presume that your existing two birds are a cock and a hen, and that, taken on balance, they are also the best of your two breeding pairs. That being so, they will soon be line birds, and you will have started the breeding season with two possible lines that are birds you have bred yourself.

After the breeding season is over, and your young birds have all completed their moult, now is the time to assess the quality of your young ones and the success or failure of the breeding season. First look at all the young birds your line cock-bird has produced. You'll find one of two things: he has either bred some birds that are as good as he or bred some that are even a little nearer the standard of excellence for that variety. Either being the case, your hen has proved that the genes controlling all his good points are dominant, and that he is an invaluable stock bird. If, on the other hand, on going through all your young birds you have some that prominently carry no good features of their father, the genes that control his points of excellence are all recessive and are not reproduced in his young. He must consequently be discarded from your breeding team, even though he can still be a show bird.

You should now repeat this process with all the young ones bred from the line hen. If, after having done so, you cannot find any that are as good or better than the hen, then all her genes are recessive and cannot be reproduced in her young. You must discard her, too, from your breeding team. This point emphasises the importance of starting to line breed with at least two pairs of birds.

You can offset any chance of breeding from a line bird that carries recessive genes if you let this particular young bird pair one season to one that has had a previous breeding season and has proved itself to carry good, dominant genes. Any fancier who is introducing new, outside birds into a bird room of quality stock, is advised to test mate the new arrival, especially so if it is a cock-bird that will almost certainly be paired up to several of his best hens. If the new cock's genes are all recessive, then it will have been a wasted season for all those good hens.

Let us suppose that your number-one line bird, the cock, has produced some good young ones. From these you should select the best young hen, and the following breeding season pair it back to its father. When breeding season number two is completed, and all the young ones completely moulted out, you repeat the selection process again. If you have once more been fortunate to breed another good hen, when breeding season number three comes round, you pair your original number-one line cock to its youngest daughter. When that breeding season is over, and once more all the young birds have completed their moult, you again assess the quality of all the young. Those young who have not held their own for type and quality are disposed of.

From the remaining young birds you select the best one, irrespective of its being a cock or hen, and that one will be used as your line bird the next breeding season. You should then pair it up to one of its first cousins – one that does not have any weakness or failure of excellence the new line bird has.

From the first breeding season that you commence line breeding, if

Original outstanding

Male   Female

Here we mate the outstanding cock-bird (shown in black) to a hen (shown in white)

First generation offspring
Contains $1/2$ of the characteristics of the original outstanding male (shown in black)

Second generation offspring
Result of mating first generation hen back to original outstanding male. Contains $3/4$ of the characteristics of the original male (shown in black)

Third generation offspring
Result of mating second generation hen back to original outstanding male. Contains $7/8$ of the characteristics of the original outstanding male (shown in black)

Fourth generation offspring
Result of mating third generation hen back to original outstanding male. Contains $15/16$ of the characteristics of the original outstanding male (shown in black)

Father × daughter-type line breeding

you follow the above steps and develop an eye to pick out type and quality. If you're fortunate enough to enjoy good breeding seasons, you should establish a good stud of your own line-bred canaries – possibly in only four breeding seasons. Remember, be a true fancier, and always put your own-bred birds before cash offers. This is not, however, to say that you do not dispose of your surplus line-bred stock. And always try to help the fancier at the other end of the ladder – just as you were years ago.

There is just one thing I must emphasise about line breeding: you must only breed from birds that are in one-hundred-per-cent good

health, have very good wing and flight-feather carriage, and are completely free from any signs of scaly legs. Both greens and cinnamons
must show the correct background colour and pencilling on their backs
and sides. There must be no light colour in either the legs or feet – the
darker these are the better. There should also be no light colour in the
area of the vent, or throat.

The characteristics of your birds should be controlled by you. If you
cease to select the breeding pairs carefully, the result will be a departure
from your line of breeding. This is most effectively displayed in the
breeding room where the birds do their own selecting.

When I'm judging canaries at a show, I always give the bird in the
show cage on the judging bench in front of me a second overall glance,
from its beak to its tail, to see what it looks like for type. If the
impression is that of lacking in type, I only look to see if it is good
enough to be in the cards. On the other hand, if the quick glance reveals
excellence of type I look very carefully at it again, starting at the beak,
then the head, neck, body, back, flights, tail, legs, feet, colour and quality
of its feather, its position on the perch, the movement between the
perches, and finally how the bird has been staged – in other words, the
cleanliness and condition of the show cage, the perches, and the general
effort the exhibitor has made to ensure that the bird would be classed as
a winner. All these things take me less than half a minute, provided the
exhibitor has trained his bird how to conduct itself while on the judging
table.

This will show up directly your skill – or lack of it – in the selection
of your breeding pairs. To be successful as an exhibitor you have to
breed birds that possess a steady, relaxed temperament when their show
cage is handled by a stranger in unfamiliar places. If you breed a bird that
excels in both type and feather, but which is nervous and tense when its
show cage is handled by a stranger, then that bird will never win in a
class of thirty or more birds – even less be awarded best Norwich in the
show. Only breed from birds that are relaxed, steady, and composed at
all times.

When you visit the New Colour or Red-Factor canary sections at
shows, you will find birds that are very tense, squatting down, gripping
their show-cage perch very tightly, or constantly jumping up on their
show-cage front. The reason for these bad habits or faults is that they
have been inherited from their distant ancestor, the Hooded Siskin, and
their faults will only be bred out of these birds by carefully-selected line
breeding with birds that do have the desired characteristics.

Note: **Colour captions and colour plates follow.**

1. The Ideal Norwich Appearance

Anyone taking a long hard look at this front facial-looking Norwich will see an almost perfect appearance of an adult clear-buff Norwich hen in perfect condition. It was bred and exhibited by Keith Ferry of Northants, and at the 1986 National Cage Bird Show held in Birmingham won the supreme award for the Best Exhibit in Show.

For all those Norwich breeders yet to receive the award for the best Norwich in show, much can be learned by carefully looking at this photograph with both our eyes. Where we assess or start to judge a Norwich canary, we always start by first looking at its head and beak, and this particular photograph was taken with the bird standing in the ideal position in which to display all its points of excellence, or visible defects.

We will start with the beak. It is nice and short with the upper mandible correctly just over-reaching the lower one. Remember we are looking at an adult clear-buff hen, so the bird's perfectly clear, flesh-coloured beak gets the bird off to the correct start.

Now look at the head feathers starting at the beak. We see that they rise up from the beak, giving an appearance of the head rising up above the beak, and moulding into a broad, wide head, which has a gentle rise over the top of the head.

The hen's eyes are set in the centre of the side of the head, with the short, thick feathers rising up and outwards from the eye, resulting in the bird having a level, large and perfectly-feathered head. Now a word about the visible colour of the head feathers, bearing in mind that we are looking at a buff hen. The colour of the head and face feathers is very clear and distinct – I mention it should be in Chapter 2.

We now come to the hen's neck, and we immediately see that it is very short and in complete harmony with the head and shoulders, giving the balance of the top end of the bird – a perfect start to the so-essential John Bull appearance. The shoulders are both broad and full, setting off a deep, broad chest, with beautifully-controlled feather quality and with no tendency to any roughness. The whole outline of the body gives a very smooth and unblemished outline – a remarkable achievement with a 16-cm ($6\frac{1}{4}$-in) canary carrying so much large and dense feather, especially so when you take into account a Norwich canary's heavy under-flue feather.

The angle at which the tail was photographed clearly shows a tail with the feather lightly compacted but with each individual feather being slightly visible, thus allowing any feather defects to be seen. The tail must be short in length and in proportion with the bird's size.

While this particular photograph does not show the hen's wings, they are in fact just the ideal length, terminated at the root of the tail, and resting lightly on the hen's back, with the individual feathers in each wing lightly meeting in the centre of the back.

The legs must be well set back to enable the bird to stand at an angle of 45 degrees to the perch. The legs, feet and toenails should be a clear flesh colour, as this is a clear bird. The feet and nails should firmly grip each square perch.

It is this firm picture of the ideal Norwich that you have to carry firmly at all times in your mind's eye, especially when purchasing new stock and when you are selecting your breeding pairs. You should then be sure to pair up only best type and feather to again best type and feather. Never pair up two birds that both have the same fault. If you do so, then you will make the fault dominant in your birds. Finally, only pair a yellow ground-feathered bird to a buff ground-feather.

Photograph courtesy of Dennis Avon

2. A Yellow Norwich Cock

Here we have a lovely yellow cock, with grizzle marking on the top of its head. This Norwich would have to be exhibited in a class for variegated yellow cocks. Note that the bird is standing in a typical Norwich position, which shows off to perfection the bird's lovely width across the top of its head, as well as the rise in feather around the beak, and the fullness of the face of the bird, with a nice, neat, small, clear beak.

The neck of the bird blends in perfectly with the head and shoulders. The chest is both full and deep with not a single feather being visible by protruding outwards from the curved outline of its chest.

We can see even with the photograph taken at this particular angle that the tail is both short and lightly compacted and in proportion with the overall size of the bird. The tail feathers readily display the same depth of colour as those of the body. This is a very good example of how an expertly colour-fed and moulted-out exhibition Norwich canary should look. For an adult bird I particularly like the appearance of the legs, feet and nails, there being no evidence of an unsightly sign of scales.

Plates 1–3 clearly show just how and what colour a Norwich should look, be it a yellow or a buff-feathered bird. Note how this particular bird's legs are well set back, and help to give the bird that Norwich position on the perch.

Photograph courtesy of Dennis Avon

3. A Self-Cinnamon Norwich

Sixty years ago, self-cinnamon Norwich canaries were very popular on the show bench, and I am pleased to say that today in the late eighties breeders are again taking up this variety. Here we have a self-cinnamon unflighted yellow cock, with its darker pencilling marks on both its back and sides. It is good to see a young cinnamon Norwich that displays both good feather, colour, and type. We can see that this young Norwich has both nice, short, flight and tail feathers.

In my 150,000 miles flight around the world visiting canary breeders and carrying out judging engagements, it was during my four visits to Australia that I thought there were some of the best coloured self-cinnamon Norwich anywhere in the world.

Plates 1–3 are photographs of real, live national-show winning Norwich canaries and are not an artist's idea of the ideal. These are what you must learn to carry in your mind's eye.

Photograph courtesy of Dennis Avon

4. A Variegated Yellow Hen

This is a photograph of an adult variegated yellow hen, taken at a slightly different angle to the other photographs. Here we can see the head very clearly, and in particular we can appreciate the large amount of short, well-controlled feather that is so essential to the make-up of a good Norwich head.

In the photographs in the book all the birds excel in their heads, there is no appearance in any of the six birds' faces of any 'meanness' or narrowness, or coarseness of feather either across or above the beak. This fault is well illustrated in Plate X.

Normally you will find you can breed a Norwich that has a good, broad head. You will then have also bred a Norwich that has good body characteristics because the bird's genes controlling feather shape and quality are those that are so necessary in an exhibition Norwich canary.

The only adverse comment that I have to make about the bird in this particular photograph is about its very scaly feet and legs. This defect need not be a feature of an exhibition adult Norwich. In Plate 1 of an adult buff hen, both the toes and legs are completely free of scales as you can see, and what a beautiful example of an ideal Norwich canary it is.

All Norwich canaries must have the appearance of being completely relaxed and of being good-natured and contented canaries.

Photograph courtesy of Dennis Avon

5. A Variegated Buff Hen

Here we have a photograph of an adult, lightly-variegated buff hen, which won its class at both the 1985 and 1986 Scottish National shows. Here we can clearly see just what an ideal Norwich canary should really look like. The hen has a lovely broad neck that rises up from the beak, nice rounded cheeks, and a short and compact neck, which blends itself naturally into the body. The hen has that typical Norwich position when standing on the perch. It is possible to see a gentle rise over the shoulders and across the back.

Again we note short flight and tail feathers that are carried lightly compacted, which quickly shows up any flight or tail feather faults as well as their excellence. The legs are well set back and this in turn helps to produce the truly acknowledged Norwich position. This, plus the bird's outline and quiet, naturally composed nature, all go towards building up a picture of a dignified, gracious, very quiet-natured John Bull of a canary.

I have just one suggestion to the fancier as to how this particular bird could have been improved before sending it out to a show, and that is the appearance of scales on the bird's toes and legs. These scales appear sooner on some birds' feet and legs than others. This defect can be greatly reduced if the bird's toes and legs at the very first sign of scales are gently but firmly massaged several times a week with a solution of zinc ointment and paraffin oil.

Never buy in to your stock an adult Norwich that has badly-scaled toes and legs because this can be a genetical defect that you will in turn breed into your stock.

Photograph courtesy of Dennis Avon

6. An Unflighted Buff Hen

This photograph of an unflighted buff hen illustrates very clearly what a 16-cm ($6\frac{1}{4}$ in) Norwich hen is all about. The distinct eye is surrounded by short, very compact feathers rising up from the eye in an outwards direction, which gives the head a large, flat, but slightly round top, and we can clearly see how the feathers from the area of both the beak and the eye go to produce the distinctive head qualities so very necessary in all good Norwich.

We can clearly see the deep, broad and full expanse of the chest, with its dense, yet very well-controlled feather. It is nice to see that not a single out-of-position feather is present, and the hen's chest outline is of a single, graceful curve outline.

Both the bird's flight and tail feathers are comparatively short, gently compacted, helping to give the bird that John Bull appearance of the canary fancy. It should be noted, although this is a photograph of an unflighted buff hen, just how short and compact are its body feathers, there being no evidence of any coarse, open feather. Both the flight and tail feathers are short and compact, keeping that John Bull appearance of the canary.

When this particular photograph was taken the bird was standing completely relaxed. If it had been quietly made to work the perches first, then it would have had an appearance very similar to the bird in Plate 5 – that which will catch the judge's eye when on the judging bench.

Photograph courtesy of Dennis Avon

7. A Clear Yellow Cock

Here we have a lovely, clear yellow cock, which has been taken at a different angle to Plate 2. This shows the width or size looking down on the top of the head, with its fine, silk-like quality of its feathers, and lovely evenness of its deep colour. While the top of the head is very broad, it is not flat across the top or centre, but has a graceful rise. The feathers around both the beak and eyes rise in an upwards direction, which enhances both the size and fullness of the head.

The neck is both full and short in appearance, and very gracefully blends the head with the body, at the same time continuing to emphasise the size and width of an excellent head. The bird's back is full in shape and width and shows a gentle rounding while its chest is both full and deep, giving that distinct Norwich John Bull appearance.

Both the tail and flight feathers are nice and short and lightly compacted, which enhances their depth of colour. For a 16-cm ($6\frac{1}{4}$ in) canary, the bird displays a lovely, short, compact and well-controlled feather, there being no protruding feathers to spoil the bird's outline. The yellow feather is very good both for its colour and evenness throughout, and the beak, feet and legs are both clear and scale free.

The bird is standing completely relaxed and if it was being judged at a show, and was gently made to work the perches, it would lose that completely relaxed appearance.

Photograph courtesy of Dennis Avon

8. An Unflighted Green Buff Hen

This shows an unflighted green buff hen, a colour now re-making its presence at the larger Norwich shows. Starting with the head, the feathers round both the beak and eyes rise up and outwards to give a nice bold head. It's not quite as bold in its appearance as the yellow cock in Plate 7, but we have to remember that this is a self-green buff hen as opposed to a clear yellow cock.

For a buff hen this bird has excellent quality of feather, which clearly shows the pencilling marks on both its back and sides. This draws attention to just how short and compact are all its body feathers. The short flights and tail feathers are as you would expect to see them in an unflighted Norwich. It is nice to see a deep, full chest and body that at the same time is well above the perch. The body feathers, behind the legs, are all nice, short and closely carried to the body – not a single feather spoils a very clear and distinct outline.

As is to be expected with a self-green bird, both the bird's beak and legs are coloured, as are its toenails. While self-green Norwich are few in numbers on the show bench in the UK, out in Australia I have seen some lovely self-greens and cinnamons, the latter having very good, broad, round heads. If Australian fanciers can breed cinnamons with such good heads, why cannot the UK fanciers do so as well?

Photograph courtesy of Dennis Avon

9. A Clear Buff Cock

This is an adult clear buff cock that has the typical Norwich head and neck. The head is nice and broad with the feathers round both the beak and eyes growing both upwards and outwards, giving the appearance of the head being broad, deep and round. The head in the area of the beak shows no appearance of meanness or narrowness, and while the head appearance is of it being broad, full and round, due entirely to the quantity and size of the buff feather, there is no sign of any course, rough, buff feather.

The neck both is full and forms a very good connection between a full, round head and a broad, deep body. The buff feather, while it has plenty of even depth of colour, shows the frosting effect at the edges of the buff feather. Both the flights and tail feathers have that typical Norwich shortness in length, which sets them apart from most other type or posture exhibition canaries.

The legs and feet are showing early signs of scales, which indicates that now is the time to commence massaging them thoroughly with a solution of zinc ointment and paraffin oil, which will improve their appearance.

This particular Norwich is a little heavy in feather both between and behind the legs, and should be paired up in the breeding season to a hen similar to that in Plates 5 or 8, where the feather between the legs is very clean, short, and very well carried, with a good clearance between perch and body.

Photograph courtesy of Dennis Avon

10. A Clear White Norwich

Unfortunately we see very few clear white Norwich on the show bench today. Here is a clear white dominant Norwich adult hen. With so few of these lovely birds being bred and exhibited, it is only natural that those we do see exhibited are not the equal in type of the prize-winning yellows and buffs.

However, the white hen in this photograph is the equal of any yellow or buff Norwich for both quality of feather and pureness of its colour. All white-ground canaries are either buff- or yellow-feathered white birds.

This particular hen is a yellow white-ground bird, and in the breeding season it should be paired up to a buff cock, as the hen is very good for both quality of feather and colour. The cock must be first class for both type and position on the perch, as is the lightly-variegated buff hen in Plate 5. From such a pairing you can expect to breed young white-ground Norwich that have the excellence of both the adult hen's pure-white colour and quality of feather, and which are better in type than the hen is, due to the excellence in genes controlling type, these coming from the buff cock paired to the original white hen.

From only one such pair of birds breeding white-ground young, in only four breeding seasons you will have bred young white-ground Norwich that will be as good for type, colour and feather as any normal yellow or buff Norwich. And what a beautiful young exhibition white-ground Norwich you will have created from quite an ordinary type of hen.

Photograph courtesy of Dennis Avon

1. The ideal Norwich appearance.

2. *A yellow Norwich cock.*

3. *A self-cinnamon Norwich.*

4. *A variegated yellow hen.*

5. *A variegated buff hen.*

6. *An unflighted buff hen.*

7. *A clear yellow cock.*

8. *An unflighted green buff hen.*

9. *A clear buff cock.*

10. *A clear white Norwich.*

6
Preparing Hens for the Breeding Season

EGG BINDING

To me, the most interesting time of the year for any canary fancier is the arrival of spring – the coming into condition of our birds, the laying of the first egg, the hen's two-weeks incubation period, and the morning when you go into your bird room to find in the bottom of the nest a tiny, pink, fluffy little chick: a miracle of Nature.

The arrival of the first egg is eagerly awaited by canary breeders. It can, however, also bring the initial problems. For example, you may have noticed that one of your hens, having finished building its nest, is expected to lay that particular day. Instead, you find the bird off the nest looking really out of sorts. The hen may have the appearance of a ball of feathers – it is listless, has dull eyes, and is very heavy around the vent.

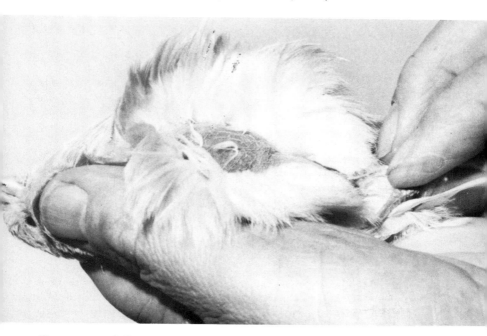

The correct way to hold a canary for examination to check condition, excess fat, etc.

Suspecting the worst, you carefully catch the bird up by its shoulders, being careful to hold it so that its body is left free from your fingers. With the bird lying on its back in the palm of your hand, you gently blow the feathers around the vent, when it will be readily seen that the hen is egg bound. To assist the bird to pass the egg she should be placed in a hospital cage that has a temperature of between 30 and 32°C (85 and 90°F).

If you do not have a hospital cage you can use a box-type cage and place it in front of a fire, ensuring that the inside of the cage does not receive the full direct force of the fire. With the help and comfort derived from the warmth, the bird should be able to pass the egg in the normal way during the next two hours. The heat should then be switched off and the cage allowed to cool to room temperature. The bird can now be returned to its cage in the bird room. If, however, she does not lay the egg, you can apply a little warm olive oil to the vent with the aid of a child's small paint brush. Egg binding does appear to happen more frequently to some fanciers' birds than others, and I feel that it could often have been avoided.

What is egg binding, and how can it be prevented? Whenever I have discussed this problem with those of my friends whose birds have experienced it, in each case they say that the hen had been given a generous supply of niger seed, and that the trouble should, therefore, not have arisen. In other words, their theory is to give the hens a fairly oily diet to keep the birds' systems supple. I personally feel that this is wrong. First and foremost it should be appreciated that hens do not require an *unduly* oily diet, because they do not function like an internal combustion engine. I would suggest that the primary causes of egg binding are that the hens are not in full breeding condition; that they have excessive internal body fat; and that hens are of a highly-nervous disposition.

Assuming these to be the main contributary causes, how do we avoid them? This is a matter of common sense, being a consistent part of our daily bird room duties. I therefore suggest the following: during the mid-winter months see that the hens are kept in a cage of sufficient size so that they have adequate wing exercise; do not use a diet with too high a percentage of starch, such as nearly all canary seeds have; and decrease the amount of plain canary seed while at the same time increasing the amount of sweet-red or black rape that contains helpful oils.

If a particular hen appears to put on an excessive amount of body fat, you should reduce the amount of plain canary seed and increase the quantity of red rape to a mixture of 50 per cent of each. Roller canary fanciers feed a very large percentage of red rape to their birds. How often do you see a fat Roller canary?

Before pairing up the birds, make quite sure that the hen really is in breeding condition. Some fanciers might feel that this is easily said but not so easily judged. Spend a quiet half hour just sitting still and watching your hens. Take note of those hens that are carrying nesting material at the *back* of the beak, and whether the colour of their shoulders and around their beaks is emphasised. Also, observe those that droop their wings and call to the cocks – nine times out of ten these are the birds in true breeding condition. Give your birds a daily bath of cold water, because all birds love a bath (or at least the majority do). Some fanciers do not introduce the cock until the hen has almost completed the nest on her own.

Often a hen will become egg bound on the second egg – be it either in the first or second round – although the first egg appears to have been laid without undue difficulty. To me there is only one explanation for this: when the yolk drops off the egg sac and commences to pass down the oviduct, collecting the white and the shell, the hen then feels a certain amount of discomfort. As the egg is laid the discomfort increases.

Those of us who have sat quietly in our bird room at about 5.30–6 am, and watched the hen in the nest that was expected to lay that morning, will have seen her half rise up in the nest, vastly extending her wings. She will remain like this for a minute or so before gradually relaxing again on the nest after the egg has been laid. I have seen a hen half standing in the nest – her body clear of the bottom of the nest – actually pass the egg; you could see her muscular movements.

In a hen of a highly-strung nature, the discomfort of passing the egg has a pronounced effect, with the result that when the second egg is on the point of being laid, the bird becomes very tense, resulting in its muscles being gripped tightly. The egg in that case cannot then be laid in a normal manner. It is only when the nervous system of the bird is soothed, and the tension relaxed by placing the bird in a warm hospital cage, that she is able to pass the egg in a natural way. In my opinion, hens that are of a highly-strung and nervous nature are better out of the breeding room.

The real answer to the egg-bound problem is proper housing conditions and feeding, only pairing up when the hen is in a true breeding condition. Additionally, one should only use hens of a naturally relaxed nature and which are also keen, sharp, and active in their ways.

When my hens start to come into breeding condition, I set the thermostat in the bird room for the artificial electrical heating at approximately 10°C (50°F). This is solely to ensure that should a sudden cold spell come during the early hours of the morning it does not create a frosty atmosphere in the bird room at the time when the hen might be going to lay her egg. To me, warm means natural relaxation, and I suggest you try it on yourself to prove the result.

Another useful point associated with the eggs is whether you are right handed or left handed. It is always advisable to try to place the nest pans or nest box at the end of the cage where you can readily put in your hand to remove the egg when it is laid without the strain or danger of breaking the egg.

DIET

When the hen is in breeding condition it is particularly important that she has a good supply of cuttlefish bone, because just prior to laying you will find that she will peck out large quantities of it. The egg-shell consists of some 85 per cent calcium, and cuttlefish is almost 100 per cent calcium. This means that the bird is not solely dependent upon the calcium within her own system. Try grating the cuttlefish bone, or better still peeling it with a knife as you would an apple. When it has been peeled it can be given to the hen in a soft-food dish and you will find that she will eat a great deal of it. After the hen has taken a bite you will see the V-shaped mark in the remaining curled-up, peeled cuttlefish that her beak has consumed. The liberal use of cuttlefish bone will greatly help to reduce the possibility of soft-shelled eggs and also, I feel, dead in shell.

Those breeders who are not able to give their breeding hens a fresh supply of soft food during the middle of the day when the weather is hot, should not use hard-boiled eggs. It is surprising how quickly hard-boiled eggs in a very hot bird room can go what I call 'off'. Most of the proprietary brands of advertised soft food have been sufficiently nutritious to cover the complete range of vitamins the bird requires, so that unless you are particularly anxious to increase the vitamin content of the soft food, it is not necessary to use hard-boiled egg. (I am, however, personally a firm believer in using it in my canaries' soft food, even in their water feeds.)

Before the Second World War, when I first started to breed canaries, the method of feeding breeding hens in those days was to give them ground-up arrowroot biscuits in one container, and in the other half a hard-boiled egg, leaving it for the bird to eat. We did not know then to put the hard-boiled egg through a sieve – that is something I have learnt to do since I first started out all those many years ago. The reason for putting the hard-boiled egg through a very fine sieve is that the resultant egg mixture is a complete mixture of both the yolk and the white, and both these are necessary if the hen is to receive the full food value within the egg.

TIMING

We must remember that there is no-hard-and-fast date in the calendar when we should pair up our birds. The time of year at which birds should be put together varies according to circumstances. There is nothing in the whole round of canary breeding that requires such a cool head – the capacity for resisting temptation – as the itching desire in early spring to pair up your birds. It is only experience that makes the breeder wise in this particular aspect. Nature, if we would but study it, has regulated all things well for the protection of both old and young birds and, as I have pointed out before, the breeder may go against Nature with disastrous results.

These disasters include such things as egg binding and also the reason our hens produce clear eggs. When a hen lays an egg it must by then have acquired all the vitamins and minerals necessary for the young bird or the embryo inside the egg to develop into a canary chick. If any are missing or they are there in insufficient quantity, that can well be the cause of dead in shell.

When our young chicks are hatched they are bountifully covered with a fine, silk, down-like fluff that is quite sufficient for the first few days when the mother keeps them closely covered. She leaves the nest for only a few seconds, in which time she will eat a little egg food with which to feed the young. However, the chicks' down becomes thinner and, just before the actual feather quills appear, the young birds are almost bare. However, by then they have grown considerably in size from when they were first hatched, so they help to keep each other warm while the hen is off the nest feeding. At this time the hen comes off the nest more frequently, and remains off for longer periods. It is now that danger occurs if the weather is really cold as the featherless young will soon be chilled. Of course, if artificial heat is available in the bird room this can, to a great extent, be avoided.

Scores of infertile eggs are another result of pairing the birds too early. This can be particularly so with the heavier breeds of canaries such as the Norwich, as was the case in a recent spring with many fanciers' birds. The symptoms of this desire to pair the birds generally show themselves on a sunny day after a period in the bird room: perhaps we have been for a walk in our allotments or fields, and picked up a sprig or two of chickweed or young dandelion leaves, having given these to our birds. They thus acquire a taste for them, and the next day we find that some of our hens are carrying their stalks and roots in their beaks about the cage. It seems to have infused fresh life into the bird room, and also into the fancier! The weather continues to be mild, and another walk is taken to gather fresh moss, and so on. Unless the fancier knows the folly of giving way to this unexpected early sign of fine spring weather, he becomes as restless as the birds.

We should remember that one swallow never made a summer, and that several fine days do not make a spring. The return of inclement weather makes us feel glad we proceeded no further than a general clean up of the cages, and an examination of nesting material and equipment. The old saying, 'more haste, less speed', should be written over every bird room door. I have known breeders lose nearly half their hens by disregarding this advice. Death from inflammation of the egg passage, resulting in egg binding, is often the penalty for bringing birds into breeding condition before the dreary days of winter have passed, especially so if no heating is available. One rule is never to pair up birds until you can see to feed them at 6 am.

From 7 pm to 6 am is a long time, especially so if you do not have any artificial lighting, and even supposing that the young ones all had full crops at 7 pm. The policy of waiting until the spring is fairly advanced will be fairly obvious. A safe rule, one based on common sense and long experience, is to wait at least until the middle of March, even if the weather is good and you live in a southern or south-western district of the UK, or until the beginning of April in the midlands or northern parts of Britain.

BREEDING

When a number of birds have been living together through the winter, the hens in one large cage, and the cocks in another, they should be looked over early in the spring. Those intended for breeding purposes should be put apart and kept quiet in the cage in which they will breed. The cocks by now will gradually be growing fresh, as I call it, and will require to be put in separate cages on their own. When they have been kept together in light cages for lengthly periods it is surprising how they will remain amicable until one or more of them begins to come into a high condition and full song. If there is any trouble in this way, the birds causing it should be removed.

Assuming that things have gone on in an orderly fashion, and that no jealously has sprung up among the birds, the breeder should find himself into early March with a good stock of healthy birds. I would advise him at this stage to switch on his thermostatically-controlled heating if he is to make a start during March or very early April. At the best March is a blustering month and April is not to be relied upon. East winds at that time continue to harass us, and winter does not depart without a struggle. In quarters made comfortable with the use of heating, the birds will soon show a desire to pair up.

Many fanciers make the grave mistake at this time of feeding their hens too richly. The amount of egg food should not be over-done. Because the cocks are in song, fanciers are sometimes under the impression that they do not require feeding up to the same extent as the hens, and the consequences of this can be infertile eggs. The month before they commence to breed, the cocks need feeding well to bring them into full breeding condition. A safe rule is to provide each bird with a half teaspoonful of soft food twice or three times a week, with the same amount of conditioning seed on the other days. The cocks will then be ready to pair at about the same time as the hens, and this should improve the rate of fertility. It's a good idea to put a pinch of maw seed into the soft food, especially for the cocks, and a pinch of niger seed for the hens will also be beneficial at this time.

When the birds are observed to be ready to breed, a nest pan or nesting box should be put in the breeding cage adjacent to, and level with, one of the perches. Place the nest pan between the two perches, the bottom of the pan on a level with them (or nearly so), and with the top of the nest about 25 mm (1 in) above the height of the perch with about 25 mm (1 in) between the actual nest and the perches themselves. This will allow the birds good standing room when they are engaged in feeding, but this is not of vital importance as the birds can, and will, stand on the nest-pan edge as often as the perch itself. Indeed some breeders, including myself, never place their perches on the cross-bar but support one on the upper cross-wire and the other on the middle cross-bar, between the door-frame and the side so that the birds fly up to the nest. As the birds grow older, the nests are transferred to a low level, approximately 25 mm (1 in) from the floor in case any of them

Left: wooden nest pan; right: earthenware-type nest pan with a gripping rim

should fall out of the nest. They will then be able to return on their own to the nest.

The location of the perches, and so on, is entirely a matter of preference for the fancier. There is, however, an advantage in keeping the top of the nest above the perch, if a perch is put near to the nest. It will then compel the hen to leave her nest more readily, with less likelihood of her dragging the young out with her, because she usually rises up and steps on to the edge of the nest pan before hopping up to the perch itself.

For the last ten breeding seasons I used only carpet underfelt as nesting material. This, of course, had been thoroughly washed and dried the year before it was used, and I think it quite true to say that my birds made some of the nicest nests they had ever made and the cost of the materials was only minimal. You must ensure that the underfelt does not include any fibrous materials, only a soft woolly build-up. If you know of anyone who is having new carpets and who will have some old carpet underfelt to dispose of, be sure to obtain a good supply.

Having cleaned out your cages thoroughly and gone over all of your nesting equipment, it is time to think about putting the birds into the breeding cages. You must decide first whether to breed from a pair of birds or whether the hen is to do all the rearing on her own–the cock is there only to fertilise the eggs. When you first pair your birds together it is necessary to spend an hour or so in the bird room sitting still and making quite sure that the birds are getting along amicably together. Occasionally one of them might turn on the other in a vicious manner.

Several seasons ago I tried something new with three or four pairs. I gave the hen the nest pan complete with nest lining, and allowed her to get used to it for two or three days. It was interesting to see the hens go inside the nest pan, spread out their wings, and scuffle with their feet at the bottom of the nest lining as though they were building a nest. When I saw them doing this I gave them a little nesting material, because until a hen begins to build her nest in earnest, she will waste most of the material given to her.

If there is moss or felt in the rack hanging up in the front of the cage and protruding through the wires, a hen will continue to pull at it. However, if she is not really in proper breeding condition she will only throw it out of the nest and scatter it about the bottom of the cage. For those fanciers who live in a large city area, I suggest that, to obtain an adequate supply of moss for your hens to build up their nest, you go to a florist where you can buy large plastic-bagfuls for a very reasonable sum. It is actually cheaper than buying nesting material, and the birds seem to build a better nest when using it.

This is all part and parcel of knowing when your birds are in true breeding condition and are actually ready to be paired up. The ideal is to pair your birds up and, after they have been together for twenty-four hours, give them a nest. This is what I have done for almost all my fifty-odd years of breeding canaries. A few days later, provide the nesting material and within a week the hen should have built a fine nest – if she is in true breeding condition.

Within another week the hen should have laid a clutch of eggs. If, at the end of ten days, the hen has neither laid nor has the appearance of going to nest, I would suggest that the best thing to do is to part your pair of birds.

A small point worth mentioning is that, before I enter my bird room, I always make a habit of tapping lightly on the bird room door with my fingers. Some fanciers appear to enter a bird room in a clumsy or noisy manner, and this could perhaps cause the hen to claw holes in her eggs when she is frightened off the nest because of the sudden and unexpected interruption.

The removal of the eggs as they are laid, and their substitution with dummy eggs, is something I was told to practise over fifty years ago, and I have always done so each and every breeding season since. This is possibly what most canary breeders do but, as I have said before, in this hobby of ours there are no hard-and-fast rules. I know of one particular gentleman who kept Lizard canaries and never removed an egg once the hen had laid it. He always seemed, however, to have a good breeding season, perhaps partly due to the fact that he used a spare bedroom as a breeding room. This would, of course, give a much more even temperature inside his breeding room.

The only argument I have heard in favour of allowing the hen's own eggs to remain is that wild birds are untouched until the full clutch has been laid and she commences to sit. However, the bird in the wild does not become broody until she has laid a full clutch and, consequently, she does not even remain near her nest during the time between the laying of the eggs and brooding the eggs. She is, therefore, in a different environment from that of a canary in a breeding cage in a bird room. A canary confined to a breeding cage can hardly be said to be in a natural state like the wild bird. Because she is never allowed to lose sight of her nest and eggs she has every inducement to sit on them as they are laid.

What retards the growth of little chicks in the nest is if they have not been fed sufficiently throughout the hours of daylight by the parent birds. Another retarding factor is if the food the parents feed them does not contain a fully-balanced diet. If the youngsters have not been properly brooded for the first twelve days, this will quickly retard the growth of the young birds.

Good husbandry must be our aim at all times to ensure the strength of the young bird goes into its body for physical growth, not diverted through sheer necessity into keeping itself alive. This is another reason why I stressed earlier the importance of using a heat of at least 10°C (50°F) or even a little higher during the actual breeding season. I know that the use of artifical heat will involve you in additional expense, but this can be well and truly rewarded in good husbandry when you see the growth and development of your young birds.

CONCLUSIONS

My approach to preparing for a successful breeding season is, therefore, first and foremost, to use only those birds that are physically fit and have not had any illness during the winter months. I do not use birds that have been bred from poor feeding hens or whose parents produced more than one clear egg per nest. These two characteristics have to be bred for just as much as you breed, for example, for a good head. I endeavour to get the cocks in full breeding condition before the hens. From mid-December to the middle of January I only give the adult birds a small teaspoonful of good-quality condition seed twice a week, increasing this to five times a week at the end of January. I also feed a little sprouted seed, and soaked seed twice a week, with the normal supply of green food.

I wonder how many realise how much the breeding results will depend upon the condition of the hen? In my opinion, she will determine the final result. The hen builds most of the nest. She has to produce a clutch of eggs and broods them for fourteen days, during which time she has little exercise or time to feed. The hen then feeds and rears the young ones for twenty-one days, ten days of which are spent constantly clearing the nest of the young ones' voids.

With such a vast amount of work to be done, I try to build up the hens' stamina and breeding condition by using the following six-point plan:

1.　Use only a good-quality condition seed and good-quality canary and rape seed, at the ratio of four to one.

2. Commence twice a week at the end of January to feed a half-tea-spoonful of good-quality soft food, increasing it to three times a week at the beginning of February, and to which has been added a little hard-boiled egg.
3. Provide a bath approximately three mornings every week.
4. Every other day feed either a little apple, carrot, or unfrosted sprout or water cress, and a little niger seed.
5. Provide plenty of good-sized pieces of cuttlefish (I have personally not used grit for many years).
6. Put three or four drops of Parishes chemical food in each individual drinker once a week.

No condition seed is fed until the beginning of March, when the soft food is reduced to twice a week and replaced by the condition seed. Before pairing up, the hen should be kept in the cage in which she will be expected to breed. This will make her feel to be in a familiar environment and will thus naturally relax her.

Equal care should be taken with all nesting materials. The nest linings (see above) should be sterilised by placing them in an old saucepan in a fairly hot oven for five minutes. The nest pans or boxes can be soaked in creosote or any other pest deterrent for a day, and then left to dry out thoroughly for a couple of months. It is a good idea to paste the nest-pan linings in the actual nest pans, thus eliminating possible hiding places for red mite. I have always used earthenware nest pans myself.

7
The Breeding Season

MATING

When both the cock and the hen are ready and in breeding condition, I pair them together in the morning – after having slightly removed the partition in the centre of the cage two days previously so that they can see a little of each other. The hen's diet is continued as before, as are the

A unit of twenty-four stock cages, or twelve double breeders

baths during the mornings (See Chapter 10). On the second day I introduce the nest pan and provide a little nesting material on the rack on the outside of the cage. As the eggs are laid I take them away each morning and replace them with a dummy egg. On the evening of the day the hen lays her third egg, I remove the dummy eggs and replace them with the hen's own eggs so that she can begin to sit her clutch.

Some fanciers like to use one cock with several hens. I make a practice of doing this so that I make the best use of my most outstanding cocks. I place the birds (two or three hens and the cock) together in a treble breeder and leave them for three to four weeks before the breeding season commences so that they can get to know each other. When they are paired up at the end of March or April they are not complete strangers to each other, and they have established a pecking order.

When I am using one cock with three hens on the same day, I run him with one hen and let him stay until they have mated. If mating does not take place in the first two or three minutes, I remove the cock from the hen's cage and put him back in his own cage for five to ten minutes. I then try with hen number two. When mating has taken place I leave them together for two or three minutes before putting the cock back in his own cage. Some years ago, using one cock and four hens, twenty-one eggs were laid by the hens and I am delighted to say that these four hens together reared twenty-one chicks.

DIET AND HYGIENE

While the hen is sitting I give her a little soft food twice a week, and a quarter of a teaspoonful of hemp seed twice a week when the soft food is not given. This, I believe, helps to maintain her strength and body temperature. When the chicks hatch out, the hen is given a little soft food twice a day for the first two days. At this stage the chicks have no digestive system of their own, and the hen will feed them with a thick liquid I call 'crop juice'. This consists of three-parts digested food the hen has picked up from what you have given her. As the chicks grow so, of course, do their stomachs, digestive systems, and appetite. The amount of food given to the hen is, therefore, gradually increased each day for the first nine days.

First I give soft food, then a little watercress, bread and milk, and finally soft food again. Each night before going to bed I put a small piece of bread and milk in the cage for the hen to feed on the next morning, as she will be feeding the chicks before I go in to feed her. On the top of the bread and milk I sprinkle a little maw seed, taking care that the bread and milk is not too sloppy. It's always worth remembering that a little food given often is worth a great deal more than two big feeds a day.

To reduce the amount of nest cleaning the hens must undertake while the chicks are only six or seven days old, I build up the bottom of the deep nests to make it easier for the young ones to void over the edge of the nest pan. When the chicks are nine days old, I feed the hens with well-rinsed sprouted seed and a little chickweed. If chickweed is not available I continue to use watercress. This gives the hen an added interest in feeding the young. Epsom salts (see Chapter 3) keeps the hens' digestive system uninfected by nest-pan voids.

At this time I also place the nest pan near to the floor of the cage, with plenty of wood shavings or sawdust placed around it. If a chick is accidently dragged out of the nest pan by the hen, or for some reason it falls out, it will then not be hurt. The wood shavings or sawdust also maintain the chick's body temperature for quite some time until you detect it and return it to its nest. When you do return it to its nest make sure you revive it by placing it in the palms of your hands and gently breathing on it for a few minutes. Nine out of ten chicks will be saved in this way unless, of course, they have been lying on the floor for too long before you find them.

By the time the chicks are seventeen or eighteen days old, the hen will often want to go to the nest again. I tie a short piece of soft string to the inside of the cage front – it's surprising how this keeps her occupied, preventing her from plucking the young.

On the evening of the twenty-first day I take the young ones away from the hen, putting a split ring on each chick for identification purposes. However, I make sure that I have seen the young ones feeding themselves from the dish placed on the floor of the cage or the feeding board fitted inside the cage door. Nowadays I keep to a single colour of ring for the legs and have the rings numbered. All young Norwich are close rung when five or six days old.

The chicks are placed in a single cage, the bottom of which is covered with newspaper. No perch is fitted inside the cage for the first couple of days. A small dish of fairly sloppy bread and milk, chopped-up egg, and a little chickweed is placed inside the cage door. The paper on the cage bottom is changed every day. On the third or fourth day, I place a very thin perch inside the cage only 25 mm (1 in) above the floor so that they can get used to it on their own.

The diet for the first week or ten days consists of bread and milk (which is gradually made less soppy each day), soft food, and a little chickweed (you can use watercress). Sprouted seed is introduced to the young when they are about four or five weeks old, and a seed hopper containing sweet-red rape is put on the cage front when the birds are some six weeks old. Both soft food, watercress, and sprouted seed are fed until the moult is well under way or, in the case of watercress, until it is difficult to obtain, although these days it is generally available throughout the year.

A show cage with one thin perch is hung on the front of the breeding cage at five weeks old. The young birds are quietly and gently handled once they have become used to going in and out of the cage. If for some reason you put your hand inside the breeding cage, do it very slowly, at the same time talking to your birds as if you were talking to your neighbour. By so doing you will retain their confidence and they will become used to your hand movement. After the young ones are taken away, the hen is left on her own for one or two days, during which time she frequently bathes. Soft food is not given to her but a teaspoon of conditioning seed is provided each day.

Never alarm the birds – always enter your bird room, especially during the breeding season, in a quiet, calm manner. A startled sitting hen can quite easily put her toenails through an egg, or stop feeding her young. If it's necessary to catch a bird at this time of year, a sharp decisive pounce of the hand will usually be all that is required to catch a canary. Do not be in a hurry or a fluster. If for any reason you need to examine a bird's back or chest, lay it on the palm of your hand with your thumb across the bird's neck. The correct way of holding a canary without ruffling its plumage is to take the tips of the wings and the root of the tail between the thumb and fingers. If held in this way there is no danger of the bird trying to escape or causing itself an injury.

DISAPPOINTMENTS DURING THE BREEDING SEASON

There is not a breeder of canaries who does not at some time have disappointments during the breeding season. It may be that a hen fails to lay, or one lays soft-shelled eggs, or there may be long intervals between each egg. Some hens refuse to incubate their eggs, but this is something we seldom experience as Nature seems to instil this instinct into the birds. What can be most disappointing of all, however, is the hen that leaves a nest of eggs a day or two before they are due to hatch.

If this happens to you, using the backs of your fingers test the surface temperature of the eggs. If the shells feel the slightest bit warm to the skin, then mark the eggs with a felt pen and farm them out to other hens whose young are due to hatch about the same time. The growing chick in the egg will stay alive during a considerable drop in temperature, but only for a limited period.

Hens can become ill and die. Stress is often the cause of this, or they can become egg bound, often the egg binding occurring in the second round. The failure of some hens to feed their young is yet another problem, so it is always a good idea to mate up at the same time three or four different pairs of hens. This will enable young chicks to be transferred to other nests.

The breeder may ask what he should do when these troubles occur during the breeding season. You may have paid special attention to your hens from the time they completed their moult until the start of the breeding season. It is at this point that the birds begin to put on condition – in other words, put on fat, particularly about the abdomen. This serves three very important purposes: it provides a reserve of food material on which the bird can draw; in cold weather it helps to protect the ovaries; and it is the source of fat for the egg yolk when the ovaries begin to become active prior to the laying season. If a healthy hen is examined during the winter, you will find that there is a layer of yellow fat under the skin of her body.

There is little doubt that many of the problems experienced during the early part of the breeding season are due to fanciers pairing up their hens when they are *too* fat. I strongly advise fanciers never to breed from a hen that is excessively fat. If you examine a hen that is in good condition, you will notice that almost the whole of the fat has disappeared and that the abdomen is now like the rest of the bird's body. The hen is now fit and ready to breed.

Another problem is that a hen will eat its own eggs. In this case it is wise to dispose of the bird as it will never be an asset to you in the breeding room. Sometimes the cock is responsible for this. He should be removed from the breeding cage, leaving the hen to incubate the eggs and rear the young on her own.

There are also hens that will lay only one egg, and then take no more notice of the nest. They hop from perch to perch, calling to the cock for food, or they just mope about the cage. These hens, too, should be disposed of, as they are not of benefit in the breeding room – their ovaries are underdeveloped.

Sometimes a hen lays a clutch of eggs and refuses to brood them. At other times, hens sit for only part of the fourteen days' incubation period. This can be as a result of the bird not being in true breeding condition. I normally give these hens a second chance, as a sudden change in the weather or room conditions can also cause this particular problem.

It is best to separate the birds for a week or so after you have broken them up from breeding. Give the hen plain canary seed and bread and milk with glucose and maw seed sprinkled on top. A little linseed and niger seed should be scattered on the floor of the cage along with the charcoal. When the hen shows signs of wanting to go to nest again, you should re-introduce the cock in the normal way.

Barren hens are birds that fail to lay. I have known of young hens that have failed to lay during their first breeding season but in the second season have raised some fine young birds. This is probably due to a delay in the ovaries maturing – all hens have two sets of ovaries attached to the spine, but only one set will come into breeding condition.

The generally-accepted rule is that if a hen does not lay at all during a breeding season she will most probably be permanently barren. Old age is the most common reason for this, but it can also be the result of a very bad moult or severe illness. It is surprising how barren hens will go to nest and make really excellent foster parents. They will incubate the eggs put under them and rear the young birds as if they were their own.

When a hen has been sitting for six days you can examine the eggs to see how many of them are fertile. Experienced breeders do this as a necessary precaution against the hen sitting the full fourteen days on clear eggs, which can result in the loss of a possible third round. If after six or seven days, when you examine the eggs, the shells have taken on a marble appearance, you can be certain the egg is fertile and a chick will be developed in due course.

Personally, I do not overwork a hen, for as a rule she will be that much less effective in the following breeding season and also in the coming moulting period. A bird in a low state of condition when it comes to moulting will have a very trying time – Nature requires her to provide a great deal of protein from which the new feathers will grow. It is far better to let the hen sit through the full incubation period – even on the nest of infertile eggs. Allowing a hen to sit out the full, natural sitting period will prevent the next clutch of eggs coming along and being formed on the ovaries too quickly. When a hen is not allowed to sit out the full incubation period, the next clutch is often infertile, because the bird has been forced to lay again too soon before the mating can have had its necessary effect.

If, in a nest of four or five eggs, one or two are infertile, they should not be removed. When the young ones of the clutch have hatched, these eggs will help to support the little chicks in the bottom of the nest. The eggs can remain in the nest until the young are sitting on the edge of the nest pan.

If the hen is in perfect breeding condition, is not too fat, and lays the eggs at the correct intervals, it is the cock-bird we must look at for the cause of infertility. Examine him carefully to see if he has reached full breeding condition by gently blowing on the feathers of the abdomen just below the breast bone. If he is in full breeding condition, the abdomen should be a little shrunken and the vent should obtrude distinctly from the body. If the abdomen is bulging and yellow, place the cock-bird in a flight cage and give him a little rape seed, canary seed, and plenty of green food, including sprouted seed and dandelion with both leaves and split roots. When this excessive fat has been reduced, the cock should be able to fertilise the eggs and return to the hen.

If the cock appears to be in good breeding condition, check whether the feathers around the bird's vent are too thick and long, which can prevent a successful mating. Trim as much of these feathers as you think necessary, being careful not to cut away any of the actual guide feathers. I do this to all my cocks and hens during the first week of February, before I put them in their breeding cages. If you are uncertain which are the guide feathers, you should first seek the advice of an experienced canary breeder. Needless to say, great care should be taken not to cut the actual bird with your scissors.

Another cause of infertile eggs can be insecure perches. Yet another is the hen that insists on sitting on the nest and calling to the cock when she wants to be mated.

When the young birds are about ten to twelve days old, the breeder must be on the watch for any signs of the hen beginning to pluck the chicks. This usually takes place during the latter part of the first round, and is one of the most annoying things that can happen during a breeding season. You will find that the odd hen will pluck one or more of its young in order to start building a second or third round. In this case, either separate the young ones by using a wire slide in the cage – so that the hen can continue to feed them – or make use of an anti-peck spray.

Breeders will appreciate the necessity of taking a careful look at all the new nests being built to check they are not being lined by feathers taken from the young birds. Should a hen start to pluck the young birds it will continue to do so unless you take immediate action to stop it. You will find that not only does it pluck out the feathers but also the new quills as they grow out of the skin. I have found that this can be stopped by tying a 15-cm (6-in) piece of soft string to the inside of the front of the cage near the perch. This will often distract the hen from feather plucking.

It is not just the hens that develop this mysterious habit, cocks are equally guilty of the practice. When these cases occur the same precautions should be taken. If you are certain that only the cock is doing the feather plucking, remove it from the breeding cage, returning it four or five times a day so that it can mate again with the hen. After the mating has taken place, the cock should be put back in its own cage. You will find that by doing this the hen will successfully rear the young ones, and when she comes to lay her next round of eggs they should all be fertile.

I have found that the habit of feather plucking occurs most frequently when four, five or six young birds are housed in the double breeder to moult out together. In this case it can take on a much more serious form – the offender not contenting itself with plucking just the small feathers but also plucking the strong quill feathers from the birds' wings and tails. When these strong quills are growing they are full of liquid blood and if pulled out they will bleed. This generally occurs before the feathers are fully grown. The culprit causing this should be removed at once. It is usually easy to detect the culprit as it will have traces of blood on its beak and face, and all its own feathers will be intact.

If young birds beginning to feed themselves are troubled with diarrhoea, stop their green food immediately. Be sure that all the food is clean and sweet, that the water is pure, and the drinking vessels spotlessly clean. One drop of castor oil placed directly into the beak will clear up the birds' bowel trouble. If the birds are on soft food, add to it at each meal sufficient arrowroot to cover a one-pence piece. A little warm water added to the drinking water is also beneficial, or the water can be replaced with strong cold tea for a couple of days.

If the young birds take on a puffed appearance, their diet should be restricted to plain seed, plus a small amount of bread lightly soaked in milk, mixed with glucose, and covered with maw seed, made freshly each day. About ten drops of tincture of rhubarb should be added to about a cup of drinking water until the birds regain their normal appearance.

There is nothing more disappointing than the failure of a hen to hatch out fertile eggs. This may be due to the following conditions: a lack of moisture; a failure on the part of the hen to turn the eggs in the nest while they are being incubated; and a lack of vigour in the parents so that all the necessary vitamins have not been included in the egg when it was laid. Free use of baths will prevent the first cause and the second can usually be avoided by placing a piece of cardboard on part of the cage front to shelter the sitting hen.

8
The Egg and its Development into the Chick

THE OVARIES AND THE FORMATION OF THE EGG

All canary hens have two sets of egg-producing ovaries, one on each side of the spine, but it is only the left one that develops from a dormant state into a reproductive state, looking, when it does, like a tiny cluster of grapes. The ovaries are the means by which a canary hen produces the yolk of the egg. When a hen is in full breeding condition, her now fully-developed lefthandside ovaries contain a chain of tiny yokes. These vary from a very tiny, pinhead size to a fully-developed yolk size.

A canary egg consists of the following five principal parts: the shell; its membranes and air space; the white; the yolk; and the tiny, flat, germinal disc on the yolk, which was created when the pair of canaries mated. If you gently break open a newly-laid canary egg, with the aid of a magnifying-glass you will see this small germinal disc from which the chick will be developed. Each egg yolk, with its two attached germinal cells, is contained within a thin, transparent ovisac, and connected by a narrow stem to the ovary. The two flat germinal cells, one from the hen and the other from the cock-bird, already contain half the chromosomes from which the future chick will obtain all its characteristics, be they for type, feather, colour, sex, and so on. When the cock and hen mate, these germinal discs create the future chick. As the yolk becomes fully grown, its enclosing membranes become thinner round its greatest diameter, which then shows a pale, coloured zone called the stigma. It is here that the fully-matured yolk sac ruptures. The newly-released yolk and germinal cells – still protected by their thin, delicate membrane – enter the funnel-shaped opening of the oviduct or egg passage. This is the start of the egg acquiring its layers of egg white. When this stage is completed, while still in the ovary duct, it receives finally a deposit of calcium carbonate, which forms the egg-shell. The canary expels the egg, pointed end first, from her vent. The surface of the egg, when laid, is moist and of the same body temperature as the hen.

THE STRUCTURE OF THE NEWLY-LAID EGG

The structure of the egg is much more complicated than the average fancier visualises. The shell itself is made up of tiny prismatic particles that comprise a mixture of phosphate of lime and animal mucus, so arranged that the actual shell is porous. Considering its weight and size it is remarkably strong – a particular feature of the shell's prismatic nature. It is the same with a poultry hen's egg, which – when done by an expert – can be thrown through the air.

Canary eggs are irregular in shape, with one end broader than the other. If an egg is rolled along a flat surface, it will roll in a circle. An incubating hen on a nest of four or five eggs will, occasionally place her beak below an egg and gently lift it, to turn it through a part circle.

Take a poultry hen's egg and crack the shell against the side of a basin. Place both your thumbs in the crack in the shell, and move it apart with your hands over the basin. The shell separates, leaving the contents in the basin. You will see that at the opposite ends of the albumen are two slightly opaque condensed cords of albumen. These are called the chalazae. When the egg is intact they are attached at opposite ends of the egg to a very dense layer of albumen, which envelops the inner fluid cover of the yolk. Their purpose is to act as a kind of balancing weight, which makes it possible for the yolk and its germinal discs to be in an upright position at all times. Thus, when the sitting hen turns the eggs with her beak, the yolk maintains its upright position. It can be seen from this just how very carefully the egg is balanced, with the germinal cells uppermost at all times in the albumen. Another explanation for this behaviour is that the germinal cells are very slightly lighter than the albumen, and are thus able to float uppermost at all times. It is, however, separated at all times by a layer of albumen, which allows it to move very gently away at the least disturbance. Rarely does it fail to do so, and when this does occur the chick's development ceases.

While eggs are away from the hen's nest we should ensure that they are kept in a shady, even-temperatured part of the bird room and turned through 180 degrees several times a day. There is a sound scientific reason for this. When the egg was laid it gradually lost its mother's body temperature and took up the air temperature of the bird room. When this takes place the germinal growth ceases until the yolk again reaches the hen's body temperature. The construction of the egg albumen and yolk are comparatively dense, and are thus slow to both lose and recover their temperature. From this it will be seen why it is necessary to keep the removed eggs in a cool part of the bird room. Should you leave the eggs in a position that is exposed to sunshine, while the sun is shining on to the removed eggs it will further the germinal disc's growth. When the sunshine disappears the disc's growth again ceases. If this is repeated four or five times each day, for possibly the three days the eggs are removed from the nest, it will quickly kill off the live germinal discs, so that by the time that you replace the eggs in their nest on the third evening, the eggs' germinal discs will be dead in the shell.

We should also remember that the egg-shells are porous and that this can be a reason for possible evaporation. This could mean that the germinal disc, as the albumen slowly dries up, adheres in the wrong place in the egg-shell. So once again be quite sure to turn your eggs several times a day.

The egg yolk is enclosed within a very delicate vitelline membrane. The yolk is composed of both white and yellow cells. Take a poultry egg and hard boil it for ten or twelve minutes. Let it cool and then shell it. Cut it in half. It will be readily seen that there is a flash-shaped nucleus of centre white yolk, round which are several concentric layers of yellow yolk. When examined under a microscope you will see thin layers of white yolk cells among the yellow layers. On the top of the yolk rests the blastoderm, in the form of a very small disc. When this is examined under the microscope it is seen to be a tiny disc that consists only of the hen's and cock's now-fertilised disc. It is whitish all over, except for small clear spots on its surface. It is from the clear spot that the fertilised chick will grow, once the cock-bird has fertilised the egg. Not all the fertilised eggs a hen lays will go on to mature to chicks. There are a number of reasons for an egg developing dead in shell:

1. If the porous egg-shell, which is more porous at its broader end, is pierced by the hen's toenail. This is the main reason for cutting off the sharp, pointed end of the hen's toenails. The shell pores are there to allow the passage of respiratory gases and to control the rate of evaporation of water.
2. Should an egg have an imperfect chalaza, this can result in the germinal disc coming into contact with inner-shell membrane.
3. A very po rous shell can be the reason for the entry of tiny germs, especially so if the egg is dirty or wet. The porosity of an egg varies considerably with the many different forms of bird life.
4. If an egg has been laid that does not contain all the necessary vitamins this in turn will lead to the death of the chick at some stage of its development. This is why I stress the importance of the birds being in full breeding condition and of feeding granulated charcoal to all of your canaries, as it contains many different trace elements.
5. If – should it be the case – the yolk does not remain in its proper position when the egg is turned, and it floats more strongly up against the inner skin of the shell becoming stuck in that position, in extreme cases the yolk can be ruptured. This is one of the reasons for turning the eggs.

THE DEVELOPMENT OF THE CHICK

Once you have returned the eggs to the nest and the hen has settled down on them, the real incubation period commences. Some fourteen days later there will be little pink chicks in the nest, so rapid is the growth and development inside the shell. If you look at a photograph of the inside of the fertile egg after the hen has been sitting on her eggs

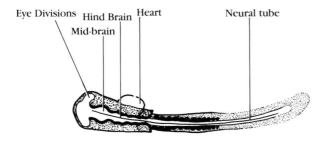

Eye Divisions   Hind Brain   Heart   Neural tube

Mid-brain

Thirty-six hours of incubation, showing eye divisions, mid-brain, hind brain, heart to one side, and completion of the neural fold down the whole length of the embryo

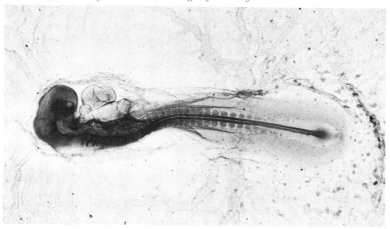

Seventy-two hours incubation. The body has turned on one side, the head and eyes are distinguished, the heart is a large bulge in chest region. The tail bud is just forming and blood vessels are clearly visible

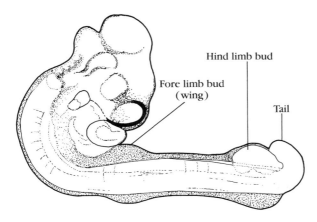

Hind limb bud

Fore limb bud
(wing)

Tail

Sixth day of incubation

for only twenty-four hours, you can clearly see the chick's initial stages of development in the embryo. The central germinal has now become oval in shape, and the outline of the headfold is visible. The blood vessels are beginning to spread. After only thirty-six hours of incubation, the eye divisions in the headfold are visible, as is the first outline of what will be the heart, to one side of the embryo. The central fold down the whole length of the embryo is now complete. After only three complete days of incubation, the tiny but enlarging embryo, enclosed in the amnion, can also be seen, as can the fine blood vessels on the surface of the yolk. The eyes are now visible as two dark spots, and there is a slight movement in the pulse beat of the heart. After four days of incubation the ear vesicles are forming and the heart is now dividing into ventricles and auricles. Both the fore and hind limbs and the tail can be seen.

By the end of the sixth day – the half-way period of incubation – the allantois can be seen as a bag or sac protruding from the navel and independent of the yolk sac. It is also possible to see the growth of the wings and legs in the form of buds, which are visible on the surface of the body. The blood vessels have now extended throughout the egg-shell – so much so that an experienced fancier can tell at a glance (without touching the egg) if it is fertile: the shell now appears to be opaque. By day nine the allantois is flat, and spread out between the outer and inner layers of the amnion, from where it gradually extends until it surrounds the now just-growing chick between the outer shell and the membrane of the egg. The allantois, with its capillary blood vessels, acts as a temporary lung, distributing oxygen it receives from the air through the porous shell to the chick's blood. The chick is not able to use its own lungs until it is at the point of chipping the shell.

This rapid daily growth and development proceeds only because of

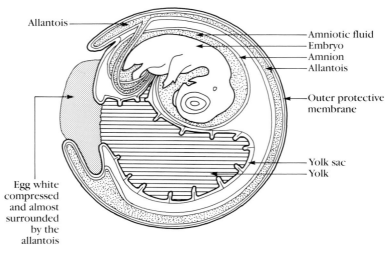

Organs of the embryo on the ninth day of incubation

Young chick two days before hatching

body temperature of the hen. All the required nutrients and vitamins are already built into the egg before the formation of the egg-shell. This again illustrates how very important it is that we do not pair up our canaries until they are in full breeding condition. By the end of the tenth day, the chick has its down-like feathering, and movement of its body can be detected. While I do not recommend you to do this, it really is most instructive for a fancier to see an egg that has been incubated for ten days to have its shell very carefully opened. The rapid rate of development can then be appreciated.

By the end of the twelfth day the tip of the chick's beak will have developed a small, fine shell-cutting tooth. Within a few hours this will enable it to break through the membrane that separates it from the air sac. The chick can then, for the first time, breathe air. At this stage the chick's blood gradually ceases to flow into the allantois, which has now completed its purpose and is no longer required. We have now reached the stage where the chick is about to break out of its shell.

With its now rapid body movement, and pressing its beak's cutting tooth against the inside of the shell, slowly an opening is made. This

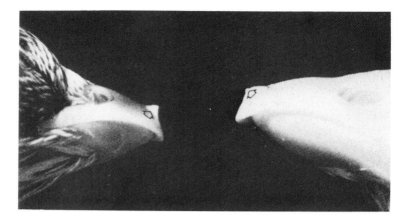

Shell-cutting tooth of unborn chick

action is frequently repeated until the shell cracks and the chick's wet head is exposed. The air invigorates the chick to fresh efforts until the shell is broken apart at the larger, more porous end. At this stage most of the hatching has been completed. The chick takes a rest to recover its strength, and then it removes the rest of its body from the shell, to lie uncurled, wet, and exhausted under the warmth of the hen's body. An hour later we have a pink, fluffy, live chick in the nest – less than fourteen days since the eggs were first sat on by the hen.

Just before the chick commenced to chip its way out of the shell, its body absorbed the remaining yolk and its curled-up body occupied the whole of the inside of the shell – its head tucked into its body at the broad end of the egg-shell. In this position it was able to press the beak's cutting-tooth frequently against the inside of the shell and press its feet against a different part of the shell. After a few hours of co-ordinated effort, it was possible for the beak's cutting-tooth to cut through the now lightweight shell. While all this is taking place, faint cheeps can be heard from the chick as it talks to its mother. There are intervals of quiet with no movement occurring as the chick takes a rest ready for making further exertions to free itself by turning its head sideways, allowing the tooth to break through the shell, little by little. This action can take between twelve and twenty-four hours.

On finally hatching, the young canary chick looks disappointing in appearance as it lies still in a moist condition, all its fluffy down yet to dry out. After an hour's rest under the warmth of its mother's body, we have a lovely little pink chick with its body and head covered with fine, silk-like down. The wetness was due to the water in which the chick had been living until it hatched.

Canary chicks are very dependent on their parents for warmth, food, and cleanliness for the first few days of their lives. After ten days, with their feather quills growing quickly each day, they are only dependent on the parent birds for food, as their self-generated heat keeps them warm when there are two or three of them in a nest.

9
Rearing the Chicks and Sexing your Canaries

REARING THE CHICKS

Feeding
When a hen's young are only a few days old, a good feeding hen will feed her chicks little but often. If you stay in the bird room while the hen is feeding the chicks, you will see that when they have had sufficient the hen sometimes visits the seed hopper for a few minutes. This is the time to take a quiet look at the chicks in the nest. You will notice that their necks are full of food, and that the transparent, stretched neck will clearly show that the hen has fed them with digested semi-liquid food.

As the chicks grow, so does their demand for food. The hen gradually changes their diet from digested food at one day old, to fresh soft food and soaked seed when they are nine days old. It is wonderful how a hen knows just when and what kind of food her young require.

It is always interesting to look inside a nest that contains your newly-hatched chicks. To me they look like a cluster of tiny, hairy caterpillars. If you give a gentle chirp like the hen, or tap very gently on the nest, the four chicks untwist their heads, beaks wide open, asking to be fed. On the top of their heads and backs stand their lovely, fluffy, down covering, and the chicks give you a feeling that all is well with them. The breeder must not interfere with the hen more than is possible – it is the hen's natural instinct to feed her young, and for the first three or four days to brood them closely.

At this stage you will have to increase the quantity of the soft food you feed to the hen, as the young chicks' appetites increase daily, this in turn seeing a rapid increase in their daily growth rate. I now start to feed the hen a little green food that will remain readily available, such as young rape-plant leaves and its yellow flowers. If you live in a large city centre, then you can feed watercress, which is a rich source of vitamins. As the days are now becoming longer and warmer, care must be taken to ensure that no stale food of any kind is left in the breeding cage.

Dealing with voids
When the young chicks are eight days old, I put a half a teaspoonful of Epsom salts in the drinking water and stir it well. This is repeated for the next four days to ensure that the hen's digestive system is not

·*Canaries at three days old*

Young bird showing feather growth

adversely affected by clearing the young birds' voids.

When the chicks are six days old I try to ensure that their voids are solid and not loose and wet. This will adversely affect her system as well as soiling her breast feathers. Any fancier can control the state of the young ones' voids by doing two things: ensuring that the soft food is crumbly and not over moist; and feeding a limited amount of clean, dry, fresh green food. I particularly try to feed the yellow flowers from a growing rape plant. This is very nutritious and the hens are very fond of it. It also gives them the urge to feed their young.

From the day the young ones are covered with hairy fluff, I always find it very interesting to guess what their colour and markings will develop into. If the down of a day-old chick is dark-coloured, it will develop into a green or three-parts dark. You can see a change in the young every day.

The mother or hen, even if she is not a very good feeder, will usually keep the nest free from voids, but should she not do so, then they must be removed each time they are fed so as to avoid their vents becoming covered by adhering excreta. Should this adherence occur, it should first be softened with warm water and then gently removed using your first finger and thumb. No young bird will thrive and grow if this vital organ is not kept free and clean either by the hen or the breeder. Some adherence of excreta round the top of the nest is of little importance, provided it is not in a semi-liquid state. If it is, carefully check the condition of all the feeding hen's food.

The hen's refusal to feed the chicks

These are the duties of a good feeding hen, and we can readily appreciate the vast amount of work a hen has to do in rearing a nest of three chicks. When young birds in the nest are constantly being fed a well-balanced diet, you will quite easily see their daily rate of growth. But it is possible that the hen will positively refuse to feed her young at all, or only after such long intervals and in such a half-hearted way, that the experienced fancier will soon tell when he looks in the nest. Instead of seeing young birds with full crops, plump breasts, and heavy abdomens, he finds the young with empty crops, their skin a reddish purple, and all the chicks close together trying to retain their body temperature. It is time to take immediate action.

There are two alternatives: either they will have to be hand-fed every hour from sunrise to sunset; or they will have to be fostered out to other feeding hens. Hens failing in their feeding of their young generally seems to occur when the young ones are nine or ten days old, and it is at this age that you can put a split celluloid ring on one of the chick's legs for identification purposes when a nest has to be split up. The rule you must follow with all your feeding hens is not to interfere with her. If she persists in sitting on the nest, then try enticing her off by giving fresh dishes of soft food and sprouted seed, even replacing her green food with fresh. This action, along with a little patient waiting on your part, normally produces the desired result.

However, for young, quickly-growing birds in the nest to have their growth rate held up is a very real retrograde step in their development. If the chicks are only two or three days old when this happens, then the following procedure should be followed: obtain some hard-boiled egg yolk, then using the handle of a teaspoon add to the yolk a mixture of water and glucose, mixing it all together until it is nice and creamy. This can now be fed to the little two-day-old chicks either by using a hand feeder or a pointed matchstalk. For most fanciers this can only be an emergency week-end effort, as it has to be repeated every hour, fifteen times a day, so if the chicks are to survive then they will have to be fostered out.

There is no difficulty in persuading a healthy young chick to open its mouth – this is almost the very first thing they do in life, and they never

Two young Norwich at ten days old

seem to forget it. The only difficulty is feeding them fast enough. When a hen does not start to feed the newly-hatched chicks within an hour of hatching, never interfere with the chicks until they are twenty-four hours old, because the yolk absorbed into their stomach is sufficient to sustain them for that time. We should give the hen a fair chance of feeding them for herself. After that time the very youngest birds can be fed in the way described, and if attended to like this at intervals, can be kept alive until the hen commences to feed.

Those fanciers who are able to visit their bird room frequently in the breeding season have a much greater chance of taking action when it is required of them. Where breeding birds have to be left from 6 am to 6 pm it will be readily seen that both the birds and the breeder are at a severe disadvantage. Those of us who are able to spend half an hour in the middle of the day with the birds will find this a great help.

In many households there is very often one member of the family who will have a little time to spare. Introduce them to your bird room and show them just what it is that you would like them to do. A canary breeding room is, even to a lay person, full of interesting goings-on, with Nature being at its most interesting and exciting time of the year. There is nothing so engaging as seeing the day-to-day growth and development of three or four young chicks in a nest. I'm sure that no temporary assistance you might have would ever allow a young bird to die without a great effort being made to save it. These so-called press-ganged assistants can be tomorrow's most ardent of fanciers.

Diet

With a nest of growing young birds to feed it is very essential that the hen is fed a well-balanced diet consisting of soft food, sprouted seed, and fresh green food. In November 1982, when I judged the Border section of the 34th National Show of the USA, held in Pittsburgh, Pennsylvania, I met several fanciers who told me that they put finely ground-up canary seed in their feeding hens' soft food to increase the amount of protein fed to the young ones in the nest. The following breeding season I tried this idea out on three feeding hens, and their young ones were all certainly very healthy, well-made young canaries.

We will presume that your feeding hen is a model mother and that all you have to do is to ensure that at all times she has a ready supply of fresh, crumbly soft food, a full dish of freshly-sprouted seed, and a small, but frequent, supply of her favourite green food. I always like to offer to my feeding hens a few dandelion seeding heads from which I've cut the long fluffy tops with a pair of scissors. Another food I give them twice a day is a dish of bread and milk, from which all the surplus milk has been removed and the bread lightly covererd with maw seed.

It is interesting to look back some fifty years ago to the early 1930s, when it was commonplace to see nests with four or five healthy young chicks. In those days canary fanciers fed their rearing hens and young birds a diet that consisted of half a hard-boiled egg in a soft food dish, another dish containing bread and milk, a third dish with crushed

Chickweed

arrowroot biscuit, and a generous supply of seeding chickweed. I am convinced that the finest and most nutritious food on which to rear young canaries is seeding chickweed.

Over fifty years ago, when I first came into the fancy, chickweed was to be found in abundance in all market gardens, and in those days there was no such thing as pesticide sprays. All you had to do was to pick up a hessian sack, get on your bike, and off to the market garden for a week's supply of chickweed – the cost in money terms was nothing, and the fancier had some healthy exercise. Life then was not so complicated as it is today, and if my memory is right, the feather quality of the birds was better than it is today.

In the UK it is the accepted thing for fanciers to purchase all their required soft food, but in Australia it is just the opposite. A very successful breeder and exhibitor of some 350 young canaries comprising Norwich, Borders and Glosters mixes the following soft food, which is both cheap and very readily eaten by all his canaries:

> 6 cups of wheatgerm
> 2 cups semolina
> 1 tablespoon skimmed-milk powder
> 1 tablespoon brewer's yeast (vitamin B complex)
> 1 tablespoon soya flour
> 1 cup *ground-up* starter pellets
> 1 tablespoon salt
> 2 tablespoons raw sugar

This is mixed and kept in a plastic container ready for use. To make up your daily requirement of soft food, grate up finely one hard-boiled egg for every six feeding hens into one cupful of dry mixture, add a little maw seed, and then mix together thoroughly with a fork. The mixture should be like fresh breadcrumbs but if it is a little dry, add some finely-grated carrot. This diet is fed to all the birds one month before pairing up commences. Always remember, you only get out of the nest what you see on the perch!

RINGING

Ringing canaries is a practice that should be carried out by all breeders, which in return will supply him with a constant record of the bird's history. To do this, turn the bird on its back in your left hand, and with the right hand pass the ring over the front claws, up the leg and over the hind claw, which is then allowed to come back into position. The ring will then be safely on the leg. The usual age for ringing the birds is five to seven days.

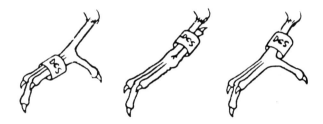

Ringing

If the rings are fitted before the female has finished cleaning the nest, it is possible that she will succeed in ejecting the offending ring from the nest – with the chick attached. It is better to ring the birds late in the evening when the light is starting to fade and the mother is less likely to spot the rings. Even so, it is always necessary to check after the birds have settled for the night that no chick has been ejected.

In the event of a chick being found on the floor next morning, even if it appears cold and dead, all need not be lost. The chick should be cupped in the hand and warmed by the breeder exhaling warm breath on to it. Unless the bird has been on the floor for a considerable length of time, it will usually revive and can then be replaced in the nest.

SEXING YOUR CANARIES

Sexing young canaries is not the easiest of tasks. This is especially so with young nest-feather birds, although I personally try to predict which ones will be cocks and which hens before they leave the nest! It is a difficult thing to forecast sometimes even after they have completed their nest-feather moult, but even so there are various useful guides.

103

As the young birds reach five weeks or more old, at this young stage you can see them making their first attempts to sing, thus disclosing their sex. On the other hand, you can have young birds that have fully completed their nest-feather moult but have given *no* indication as to their sex. Do not at this early stage despair – sexing is an exercise where even the expert makes mistakes.

Many years ago, before the Second World War, I asked an old canary breeder who had spent a lifetime breeding various types of canaries how he was able to tell which were the cocks and the hens among the young birds he had bred. His answer was that there was only one sure way, and that was if it laid an egg, it was a hen! This particular subject is only one of the many that, taken collectively, go to make canary breeding such an interesting hobby.

The answer I was given all those years ago was perhaps not what I had expected to hear, but any fancier who has bred canaries will know just how true it is. I can still remember a bold cock-bird that had a lovely mellow song, and that had twice won the unflighted variegated yellow cock classes for me at members' local club shows. The following April when, by pure chance, it was caged up with another buff cock, it laid four eggs, rearing me three young chicks. It was an excellent breeding and feeding hen. Until the first egg appeared, neither I nor any of my fancier friends who had seen the bird before had the slightest doubt that it was a cock.

Physical appearance
There are, of course, the famed Japanese sexers of young birds. I am thinking in particular of the sexing of day-old poultry chicks, but their technique, believed to be based on examination of the genital protuberances, or papillae, in the vent, is of no use to the ordinary canary breeder. Nor are the mechanical devices, based on the same principle, and which are used extensively nowadays by large-scale poultry breeders.

Even with birds the size of poultry chicks, it is a different and tricky operation for anyone but those who have the specialist knowledge and training in knowing precisely what to do. So far as I know no instrument small and delicate enough for use with canaries has ever been produced, and here we must not overlook a bird's susceptibility to sudden death from shock during handling. Such a device could well be impracticable.

The ritual of taking a quick look at the bird's vent by blowing the feathers aside that normally cover the vent, while looking very impressive to a novice, is of very little practical use except in late March or early April when the young birds are coming into breeding condition. At that time there should be a marked difference between the cock and hen in the shape and size of the end of their bodies in the region of the vents. In hens it becomes broad and rounded in appearance, with the vent itself in no way obtrusive. With cocks the structure becomes much slimmer, more elongated, and rather pointed, with the vent noticeably protuberant.

Before the start of the breeding season, especially so in the case of unflighted birds, examination of the vent area does not really serve any useful purpose. Some years ago a friend of mine asked me to go with him to buy three unflighted Border cocks. These three young birds were singing in a quiet manner as young cocks do when we entered the bird room. The owner was held with high respect for the impressive and self-assured way in which he was able to sex his young birds by a swift, but searching, look as he blew aside the vent feathers. However, this was only after many years spent learning just what to look for.

There are some useful guides to sexing young canaries, difficult though it is to describe processes that owe as much to intuition based on practical experience as to logical processes of thought. In general it will be found that cocks tend to be bolder in appearance and more vigorous and aggressive in behaviour than a hen. It is also found that cocks in a show cage grip and work the show-cage perches in a much more positive manner. Another telling indication is that a cock's eye will have a bold, positive look about it. Another indication of a bird's sex we can observe, especially in the case of buff-coloured feathers, is that a cock's feathers, immediately round the beak and top edge of the shoulders, will have feathers of a more enhanced colour. Most hens tend to be that little bit more round and softer in outline, and a little more docile in their manner and movement when working the show-cage perches.

The size of a canary is not always a certain guide as to its sex. In most types or breeds of canaries (except for those of the purest of a particular variety) there can be quite a considerable variation in size among birds of the same sex.

Song

As I have already mentioned, most young cocks begin to try to sing when they are only five weeks old, though sometimes so does the odd hen. The cock's performance is usually a more continuous and sustained warbling. The strength of the song can often be a pointer to a young cock – not always, however, for some young cocks can for some weeks produce nothing better than an almost inaudible gurgling note, though I have seen no mention of this in the canary literature. I still find it easier to distinguish the cocks while the young are still in their nest, and most of them even before they are fully feathered.

While watching and listening to a nest of young birds being fed, I have noticed a marked difference in the begging call of the young cocks. Their cry or sound is much more loud and strident, more clearly a musical note than the rapid squeaking of a young hen.

I do not suggest this as a fool-proof method, for I would probably go wrong the very first time anyone tried to test my ability. I have, however, for some years now used it as a workable and reasonably successful way of sexing a nestful of chicks at an early stage. It is only by trying to do so that we learn from experience and thus extend our knowledge.

After the fledglings' first moult, sexing becomes progressively easier as the young cocks come into stronger voice. But there will always be the odd singing hen to spoil the picture. It becomes possible to segregate the sexes with fair accuracy, and the behaviour of the birds one to one another can often reveal if an error has been made. The more mature they become, the less tolerant they generally appear of others of their own sex. But if the worst comes to the worst, you can always fall back on that completely reliable rule – if it lays an egg, it's a hen.

10
Feather and Moulting

FEATHERS

Feathers are the things every bird possesses but no other creature has.

Functions of the feather

Feathers are the sole means by which it is possible for a bird to fly. Feathers and muscles make it possible for the bird to control and regulate its body temperature. It is a fact that feathers are Nature's finest means of insulation, having often been used by man for that very purpose. All birds in cold weather maintain their body temperature by fluffing out their body feathers, and in so doing trapping the air, thus forming the insulation. During very hot weather in both the UK and the tropics, birds keep their bodies cool by expelling the air from between their body feathers. This allows their excess body heat to escape into the atmosphere. Many birds, including canaries, also use their body feathers to line their nests.

Most canary fanciers consider that the body feathers (or as some fanciers call them, contour feathers) are only there to give the bird type – but that is only in the fancier's mind, as we have already seen. If you look at each feather you will see that it is made up of many rows of long barbs that hook together. Body feathers are, for their size, quite strong and stiff, and therefore protect the bird's body from wind and rain, other than when a bird is bathing. The wing or flight feathers are rigid and long, for they have to carry the bird through the air.

Below the body feathers is a layer of soft, fluffy feathers, which do not have any so-called stem or shaft. The reason for this is that they are there to keep the bird warm at a temperature of approximately 46°C (115°F).

It is the bird's skin that actually provides the feather. A dermal papilla breaks through the skin, the outer layer forming the vital feather sheath or quill, the inner layer the actual feather itself. The base of the feather is embedded in a feather follicle from which the new feather will grow. As long as the feather is alive and growing its soft central cavity is fed by food-and-pigment giving blood vessels. Once the feather is fully grown, has lost its sheath, and is fully expanded, it hardens. The food supply now ceases as growth is completed, and the feather is considered dead. You will now appreciate why I recommend the frequent use of a shallow bath when birds are in moult. This assists in helping the bird to

A bath

shed its old feathers; the growth of new feathers; and, as the new feather grows in a protective sheath, a bath assists the new feather to discard this, allowing it to continue to grow unhindered. I only fill the baths a quarter full so as not to allow the bird to wet itself too heavily. This only uses up its limited amount of strength and body heat, thus lowering its body temperature.

No bird is completely covered by feathers; there are, on all birds, patches of bare skin. The actual feathers grow in areas or lines known as feather tracks. That is why when you hold a bird in your hand on its back and blow on its chest to examine its body, the feathers part in a line leaving bare skin. If at any time a bird loses one of its feathers, it will quickly regrow, not having to wait for its annual moult.

MOULTING TIME

The moulting time is when a bird sheds all its existing feathers. This can be a very interesting, and sometimes complex, period. As I have already mentioned, a normal healthy bird will moult all its feathers once a year. Moulting is triggered by a natural process, which begins when the breeding season is coming to a close and there is a gradual change in the hours of daylight. This triggering also produces a change in a canary's sexual and pituitary glands.

Just as there is a definite time for moulting, there is also a definite sequence for the moulting out of each individual feather. Nowhere on a bird's body is this more noticeable than in the wing and tail feathers. Should there be a loss of too many feathers at one time, or uneven moulting of the flight feathers, the bird's ability to fly would be adversely affected. In the case of young canaries, or those still in their nest-feather plumage, they will only moult their body feathers when they are between eight and ten weeks old. In adult birds this will normally start in July, depending upon the state of their pituitary gland.

In my opinion, the most demanding time in a canary's life is during the moult – for both young and old birds. Both have just completed a period demanding great strength for different reasons. Nest-feather birds have had to grow and develop their bodies while at the same time growing a complete set of feathers. The hen that has produced two or three nests of young has had to build the nest, produce two or three rounds of eggs, sit each round for fourteen days, feed the young ones for over twenty-one days, and remove all the voids made by the young. She must be much reduced in her physical condition.

Without doubt, the nest feather or first moult of any young canary will determine its future as an exhibition bird on the show bench, for better or worse. Moulting is a very important period no fancier can afford to treat lightly. A critical eye should be kept on the young birds at all times to ensure that all is well with each and every bird.

MOULTING AND THE BREEDING SEASON

The adult birds' moulting time generally commences in July, but this can vary considerably according to circumstances and your bird-room management. The whole period extends over three months. With a decline in the birds' physical condition, moulting will begin. You should be able to see just where the old feathers have been moulted by the early presence of new feathers. This, of course, means the end of the breeding season for that year.

The shedding of any flight or tail feathers is the early signal for your bird to end its breeding season. From experience I have found that it is generally the cock-birds who first start to moult these feathers, and this could well be the reason the last clutches of eggs are infertile, when you have tried to take a late last round. Your birds, especially the hens, may appear to remain in breeding condition and reluctant to cease their domestic duties, but this will quickly change as their system changes with the call to moult. Even at this stage, if you have a hen who is sitting on a nest of eggs that were fertile at the time she began to moult, it is better to remove the eggs straight away, so as not to allow the hen to exhaust its strength in trying to do two things at once.

MOULTING AND COLOUR

With many nest-feather canaries there is quite often not much difference to be found in the colour of either sex, and sometimes very little difference between even the yellows and buffs in the normal type or posture canary. However, once the birds' winter feather moult commences, the colour of the new feathers is very easily seen. In the nest-feather moult, the only difference between this particular moult and all following moults is that only the head and body feathers are moulted out. The flight and tail feathers are moulted at subsequent moults. Young greens and cinnamons will not show their true colours in their wing and tail feathers until their second or first full moult. It is, therefore, advised never to part with a nest-feather bird until after its first moult. A self-green, of nice type and colour except for its flight and tail feathers, which have a tinge of brown in them, should be kept, because at its next moult the offending tinge of brown will moult out. Green and cinnamon birds only show their natural and true colours after they have had their first full and complete moult. They are at their best for colour when they are two years old. It is true to say that the best depth of green colour in a Norwich is normally found in a small bird. The reason for this is that the size of their body feathers is smaller and finer in web. This in turn means that the bird's feather is compact, resulting in a stronger shade of green. A big bird has a larger feather web, which dilutes the shade of green and emphasises the darker colours, such as broad-black pencilling on the breast and sides, which is what we are trying to avoid.

Before the birds go into a full moult, I select those adult birds I consider will be good enough to be used again during the next show season. The cocks are put on their own in a single stock cage, while the hens are put three or four to a double breeder for their moult, and left to quietly get on with it.

FEEDING THROUGH THE MOULT AND FOR CONDITION

I was once invited to give an hour's lecture (on tape) by the New Zealand Border Fancy Canary Club entitled, 'Preparing Borders for Show'. I started by saying that I always commenced to prepare my Borders for show some five weeks before they began to moult. Once a canary has moulted, it is too late for the fancier to attempt to improve either the quality of the feather or its colour. Both these qualities can be enhanced by an experienced fancier – provided he commences to feed and condition his stock five weeks before the moult commences, even though each individual canary carries its own genes that control both feather and colour. You should also take note of points made about colour feeding Norwich canaries in Chapter 1. The point to remember is that a bird that has a good, clean, quick moult is being well prepared to enjoy a successful show season.

During my four visits to meet canary fanciers from different states of Australia, when the subject of canary moulting was discussed at length, perhaps this process was best described by W.E. Dunn, who is the General Secretary of the Adelaide Canary Society of South Australia. In partnership with his wife, he breeds and exhibits Crest and Crest-bred canaries, Australian Plainheads, and Lizard canaries. He wrote that a top breeder, now a bird dealer, once told him that champions are not only lined, but also fed. By that he means moulting is a strenuous period in a canary's life. Feathers are difficult to grow. It is necessary to feed a protein-rich diet to a vegetarian – no easy task! By protein is meant fresh amino-acids readily available to the digestive system of the canary. Forget old seeds and stale food – if they are unpalatable to you, the fancier, then do not feed them to your birds. And if canaries were meant to eat meat products they would have developed teeth during their evolution.

Some of us are allergic to meat and dairy products, but we are carnivorous, and fish and chicken can be substituted. The next best method of obtaining protein is from the soya bean. You may have read that protein-enriched biscuits are supplied to third world, drought-stricken countries. How do they enrich the biscuits with protein? This is done by adding soya flour to the biscuit mixture. In the same way we can add soya flour to the soft food we give to our canaries. Prepare your normal soft food, and then add the soya flour to it, mixing it thoroughly with a fork. Do not change your normal soft food at all, just add at first a little Soya flour to your existing mixture gradually, a little at a time as your birds acquire a taste for it. Your birds will quickly acquire a liking for it, but care must be taken when feeding it as it is very rich in vegetable oil as well as protein. It is particularly good to feed to canaries who have chicks in the nest, and also both before and during the moult. It will be found to be very beneficial to feather growth and the final appearance of the feather. You should mix approximately two teaspoons of soya flour to one cupful of dry soft food. The obvious sign that you are using too much soya flour is very loose droppings. This is quickly corrected by reducing the amount given.

We should always remember that the time our canaries are moulting (or about to) is also the time when our canaries are put on the judging table, and that 95 per cent of what a judge will see and judge are feathers. This being so, always remember that preparing your canaries for show always begins before the moult commences.

A very well-respected bird veterinarian in South Australia once said that birds brought to his surgery had lost so much condition that it was in most cases too late to treat them. The bird's capacity to process enough food to recover its condition is very small, and this is why they are constantly eating throughout the day. So if they are the product of a poor feeder, suffer setbacks, or are kept in a condition of stress, then no matter what action you take now it is probably too late. They will never reach their potential no matter how well you have bred them. As the man said, champions are fed as well as lined. I have already mentioned to start to condition your birds some five weeks before they begin the actual moult. In so doing you ensure that the bird's body condition and blood stream contain those vitamins that are so necessary for both feather growth and the correct depth of colour of the new feather. When starting the conditioning period be sure to give your canaries a supply of granulated charcoal, as this contains a very wide band of vitamins, and keep this up right to the point when your birds start to develop pen feathers in their head.

You can now, if you so wish, stop giving your birds a ready supply of charcoal, for two reasons: it will avoid the newly-growing head feathers from becoming soiled by the charcoal's container as the birds pick in it for their favourite tit-bits; and as the head is the last part of the bird to moult, its body and blood stream will by now contain all the essential vitamins needed to enable it to complete its moulting out of all its new head feathers. While all this is taking place, do not forget to give all your birds a daily shallow bath. I have always made a point of doing this each morning. This is to ensure that no moulting bird ever goes to roost at night in a damp or wet condition.

All Norwich fanciers are recommended to feed their nest-feather and moulting birds a well-balanced protein diet, with a daily supply of succulent fresh green food comprising fresh, young, growing rape-plant leaves and its yellow flowers; green seeding dock; watercress; young, tender, dandelion leaves and seeding heads; sprouts cut in half; and slices of sweet apple put between the wires of the cage fronts. As I have said earlier in this chapter, a bird's body and bloodstream must contain a fully-balanced supply of protein before and during the whole of its moult to enable the birds to produce feathers like silk — not woollens. At the same time they must have depth of colour with no trace of harshness in the colour. (For a full discussion of colour feeding, see Chapter 1; for diet, see Chapter 4.)

11
Some Canary Ailments

SIGNS OF HEALTH AND SICKNESS

If you have a Norwich that has lost its sparkle and normal good health, catch up the bird and examine its body by blowing its feathers apart. Have a close look at its bare skin as it could have indications of a possible illness. The body of a healthy canary should be nice and fresh, with its breast plump and well covered. If the bird has a pointed breast bone, and its skin is a red–purple colour, or its abdomen has dark spots on it, then this is clear evidence that you have a sick bird on your hands. A visit to your local vet should be made. Taking the correct tonics and antibiotics can very quickly cure an ailing bird, and the treatment would cost only a fraction of the cost of a replacement bird – and you would still have the same blood line for the next breeding season.

I have discussed in earlier chapters how necessary it is that your bird room must be completely draught-free. The canaries' feathers can protect birds against falling temperatures, but a cold draught could be fatal to the healthiest canary.

When you try to treat or cure a sick canary always remember that the quickest acting medicine is that given in a liquid state, as it will reach all parts of the bird. In an emergency three or four drops of equal parts brandy and water put down the bird's throat can often act as a wonderful and effective cure. The use of antibiotics, only obtained from a veterinary surgeon, will quickly counteract fungi and serious complaints. Just one visit to a helpful vet can be the answer and cure to all your sick birds for several years, and the cost minimal to you.

An infectious disease is one that can readily be transmitted from one bird to another, be they either in the same cage or a different cage, and this is done through the bird-room environment. This is different from the non-infectious diseases that one bird can have, not affecting another bird. Thus influenza is infectious, but rheumatism is not. The possibility of the risk of the spread of infection is greater where a number of birds are all confined to the same cage, where they all share the same humidity, seed hopper, and water drinkers, in close-confined conditions.

A home-made hospital cage

HEPATITIS

This complaint is exactly the same as in human beings, that is, an infection of the liver as a result of the canary drinking water or food infected by virus. This complaint can be completely avoided through good daily bird-room hygiene. If you suspect that one of your Norwich is affected by hepatitis, catch up the bird, hold it with its back on the palm of your hand, and blow the feathers apart on its breast. If its stomach is a purple–blue colour, then it is almost certain the bird has a liver complaint.

Treatment
Place the bird in a hospital cage that has a temperature of 30°C (85°F), give it a general antibiotic in its drinking water, such as aureomycin or terramycin. Feed it a teaspoonful of both soft food and freshly-rinsed sprouted seed, with a little canary and black rape seed. The treatment should be warmth, rest, a well-balanced diet, and the antibiotic will effect a cure. A week of this treatment and the bird will be back to normal. Note: this was the result of bad hygiene by the fancier in the first place.

DROP IN BODY TEMPERATURE

The normal body temperature of a healthy canary is 46°C (115°F). As soon as the canary becomes ill, its body temperature goes down. When

one of your Norwich shows signs of being unwell, place it in a warm
hospital cage to make up for its loss of body temperature – this applies
to all birds.

RESPIRATORY COMPLAINTS

If good daily hygiene is applied, then you should only be troubed by the
odd incidence of respiratory complaints, provided your canary room has
a ready amount of fresh air – with no draughts or dampness, both of
which can quickly affect any of the birds. If you have a bird room that
is constructed of wood, then you should insulate it as I describe in
Chapter 3. If a bird has a cold and breathes heavily or has a discharge
from either its eyes or nose and loses its appetite, it might well be a case
of infection. Again, the first thing to do is to isolate the bird by placing
it in a hospital cage, and give it antibiotics in its drinking water. If your
bird appears to be affected by a disease of the air sacks, which can be a
prolonged illness, you should take the bird to a vet.

Pneumonia

This complaint is normally the result of a bird having been kept in a
draught, either in the bird room or while at a show. The symptoms are
rapid breathing and gasping for its breath. Here again give the bird
either auromicin or terramicin in the hospital cage drinker, feed a little
soft food and sprouted seed as well as its normal hard seed. What the
bird requires is warmth, rest, a good, balanced diet, and the antibiotics
will complete the cure. At night time catch up the bird and put five drops
of its drinking water down the back of its throat. This will ensure a more
rapid improvement in the bird's condition.

ENTERITIS

Birds that have this complaint pass frequent, very moist droppings.
Where there is a severe case, the droppings will be in a liquid form, and
the vent feathers will be soiled. The cause of this is the bird having drunk
polluted water, or eaten infected food, or green food that was affected.
Again, put the bird in a well-disinfected hospital cage as it will have lost
body temperature. Mix very finely ground-up rice with the soft food,
and in severely affected birds put a little terramicin in the drinking water.
Do not feed any green food, but feed sprouted seed. Put three drops of
castor oil down the bird's throat once a day. You will find that this
treatment will, in only two or three days, have the bird back to normal.
Afterwards be sure to disinfect the hospital cage thoroughly.

INDIGESTION

Young canaries in particular can be affected by indigestion, and show
this by vomiting their food with a jerk of the head through their open
beak. With these cases remove all the hard seed, feed only a moist cube

of bread, milk, and glucose that has a covering of maw seed, its normal soft food, and a little sprouted seed. Put five drops of syrup of buckthorn in the drinking water, and stir well. The affected bird will soon be back to normal.

ASTHMA

This does appear to affect some fanciers' bird rooms much more than others, and I feel that bird-room hygiene management does have a lot to do with it. There can be several reasons for its presence, such as draughts or a neglected cold. Birds that are adversely affected can be quickly identified by their heavy breathing. The hospital cage should again be used, and a little glycerine put in the drinker and mixed well. Be sure to feed a well-balanced diet of soft food containing a hard-boiled egg and sprouted seed. Canaries that are severely affected are best put down.

COLDS

Our canaries do develop symptoms of being affected by a cold, generally during the winter months, when the outside winter weather is very cold and damp. I partly close my bird-room ventilator while it lasts. If you find one of your birds is breathing heavily and its feathers appear loose, then that bird's body temperature has fallen well below 46°C (115°F). Again, isolate the bird in a warm hospital cage, add five drops of glycerine to its drinking water, and stir it well. Feed the bird on soft food and sprouted seed, and in two or three days it should again be its normal self.

THRUSH

This disease will normally only be found to affect the mouths of young canaries in the nest that are being hand fed. Young birds are infected while they are gaping to be fed. You will find that the edges of their beak and tongue have a greyish-white deposit. All you need to do to rectify it is to get a normal cage drinker, fill it with cold water, and put in it permanganate of potash. After feeding the chicks, put your thumb and finger in the drinker and wipe the affected chick's beak. In only a couple of days the thrush will have gone.

EYE COMPLAINTS

For any canary whose eyes have been affected by a cold or by foreign matter, there is a simple remedy. First catch up the affected bird, then gently bathe its eyes using a small piece of cotton wool dipped in a solution of boracic powder and water. Wipe the eye dry with another piece of cotton wool. Gently put a little Brolene round the inside of the eye-lid. Brolene is available in small tubes from most chemists.

Should a boil appear around the top or bottom of the eye, give it a few days to break by itself. If this does not happen, it's best to prick it gently with a sterile needle. Get someone experienced to do this for you.

YOUNG BIRDS' FEET AND LEGS

During the breeding season you will find that an occasional chick, on leaving the nest, will have its rear-pointing claw or toe pointing forward like its three front claws. This is known in the fancy as a slip claw and the bird is unable to grip the perch with that particular foot. In these cases gently catch hold of the chick using your thumb and first finger. Take hold of the forward-facing rear claw and slowly move it to its correct position. Then, using either a soft piece of wool or Sellotape, secure the claw to the back of the leg. Return the chick to its cage for two weeks, then remove the wool or Sellotape while holding the claw. You will find that the foot and claws now grip the perch in the normal way.

Sometimes, when young birds are about five weeks old, you will see that one young bird's rear claw is unable to grip the perch at all, and that the claw is at an angle of 90 degrees to its leg – this is called 'stiff hind claw'. To assist the young bird in overcoming this defect, put it on its own in a separate cage that has no perches in it. Three or four times a day, gently massage the claw with olive oil. On the fifth day tie a 6-mm ($\frac{1}{4}$-in) thick piece of rope to the bottom of the cage front, then pull the rope tight, using a drawing pin to secure the rope to the rear of the cage two-thirds the way above the bottom of the cage – this will leave the rope at an angle. Now put the affected bird back into this cage. The piece of rope at an angle – being the only perch in the cage – will encourage the young bird to start to try to use the defective claw. After three weeks of trying to grip the angled piece of rope, you will be pleased to see how much ability in gripping the perch has been recovered by the claw. You can now replace the piece of rope with two 6-mm ($\frac{1}{4}$-in) thick perches.

SCALY FEET AND LEGS

Some adult Norwich canaries develop ugly, scaly legs and feet. The cause for this can be one of two things – or even both of them. Scales can be caused by the presence of a very tiny mite, but they also appear to be hereditary to certain birds when they breed. As soon as any of your Norwich show the first sign of any scales, either on their toes or legs, then massage *both* legs and feet (affected and unaffected) with a mixture of zinc ointment and paraffin oil twice a day. After four or five weeks of the treatment, you will be pleased at the improvement.

LOSS OF BODY FEATHERS

Normally you will find that in a bird so affected, the first part of the bird to show loss of body feathers is the back of the neck. In some cases you will be able to see the bird's bare skin. This normally indicates the presence of feather lice, and the back of the neck is the one part of a canary's body it cannot preen with its beak. In all these cases catch up the affected bird and give it a thorough dusting with Keatings powder. Using your finger-tips, work the powder down, through the feathers, to the bird's skin. No more than two such applications will be necessary.

TOENAILS

Any bird that has long toenails is prevented from gripping the perch properly, and therefore it cannot work the show-cage perches. Long nails can also be a handicap to both cocks and hens during the breeding season, so each January I cut all my canaries' nails. The correct way to do this is as follows.

First catch up the bird and hold it in the palm of your hand. Then, using your thumb and first finger, hold one toe at a time. All canaries' nails have a vein carrying blood along the centre of the nail and this is quite visible. Where this vein appears to end, allow at least another 3 mm ($\frac{1}{8}$ in) and then, using a sharp pair of scissors, at this point cut off the excess nail. Should one of the nails commence to bleed, then apply iodine to the nail. This will quickly stop the bleeding by congealing the blood. Once a year, such as in January, should be all that is necessary.

GOING LIGHT

This particular complaint is self-explanatory, for as it implies the bird begins to lose body weight to such an extent that it quite quickly wastes away to a mere skeleton and dies. I have found from experience that this complaint happens to young birds more than to adult birds whose feathers appear to be ruffled. The birds are listless and inactive and are usually between six and twelve weeks old. When I first became interested in canaries nearly sixty years ago, this problem was unknown in the canary world, so to me the problem must be due to only two things: the young birds not having developed a fully-digesting system; and the fancier not feeding young canaries an easily-digested, fully-balanced diet. In my opinion it suggests too much haste by the breeder to get his young birds on hard seed. In the wild, young finches have a diet of young, very succulent seeds until they have fully completed their moult. For fifty-one breeding seasons all my young canaries have had a daily supply of soft food, soaked or sprouted soaked seed, and fresh crisp greens every day of the month, plus a dish of granulated charcoal. Going light has never affected any of my canaries. I also give all my birds at moulting time Orovite 7 (see Chapter 4).

STUCK IN THE MOULT

Many fanciers have the odd canary that gets stuck in the moult. This is sometimes the result of a bird in the moult being affected by either a draught or a shock. If this happens to one of your birds obtain four stems of saffron flower from the chemists, put them in a small pan with a large cupful of cold water, then let the contents very gently simmer for five minutes. When it has gone cold, empty the bird's drinker and refill it with the now yellow liquid. Repeat this for the next three or four days. If the bird is really stuck in the mould, hang a very damp hessian sack over two-thirds of the wire cage front. One week of this treatment and the bird will have recommenced its moult.

CORNS ON THE FOOT

A canary sometimes develops a corn right in the centre of its foot where all its toes or claws meet. These are very painful to the bird when it is standing on a perch. This problem can be quite easily overcome. First remove all the perches from the cage, then select a round perch, and cut the top of it with a knife or wood chisel into a wide and V-shaped groove. This will then enable the bird to grip the perch with its affected foot, avoiding the corn coming into contact with the perch. Next, catch up the bird three or four times a day and literally paint the corn with iodine. After only two weeks of this treatment, the red-coloured inflammation in the foot around the corn will have gone, and the offending corn will have begun to shrink and go hard. In another two weeks the bird will be able to use its normal perch again. A bottle of clear iodine should always be kept in your bird room.

RED MITE

The greatest problem facing the breeder is the dreaded red mite. In the daytime these tiny, almost colourless creatures, hide from the sunlight, but when night comes they emerge from their hiding places to gorge on the blood of the sleeping birds. This blood colours the insect red, which is how it gets its name. Just one mite discovered could mean that there are hundreds more lurking in cracks and crevices, in the nesting material, at the end of the perches, and even in the seed hoppers. It is said that a fertilised female red mite will lay 200 eggs that hatch out in twenty-four hours. In another twenty-four hours these, in turn, are fully grown and ready for breeding.

Red mites seem to prefer the blood of the tiny, helpless babies in the nest, so search for them on the inside of the linings of the nest. If you find many of your previously healthy babies dead and very pale in colour you should immediately suspect red mite. Take the nesting material out of each nest and carefully examine it. If you see any moving specks, burn the nesting material and soak the nest pan in a strong disinfectant. Remove any live canaries from each nest in turn and discard all the nesting material. Make a new nest, dust it and the nest pan well with insect dusting powder, and place the nest and the chicks in the nest pan. Return it to the cage and you will find mother soon nestles down again on her young. Paint the ends of the perches with kerosene and paint any likely hiding places for the red mite with the following mixture:

One cake of crushed camphor
Half a cup of mineral turps
Half a cup of household Jeyes disinfectant.

Stir together thoroughly until the mixture thickens. This can be put aside and used later, but will need to be stirred vigorously again. You will find it very pleasant to smell and harmless to the birds. Check the nest and perch ends each day, as the eradication of red mite is a slow process. As a precaution, spray the room each night after the birds have settled down, especially during a hot spell. Use a good aerosol spray, spraying it into the cages and the birds. This is also a deterrent for air-sack mite, which is the main cause for birds wheezing at night.

STRESS

Stress in a canary can often be fatal, especially so at the commencement of the breeding season. It can often be traced back to the mismanagement of the fancier himself. Stress factors in a canary are, in theory, much more likely to prove fatal in an inadequate environment. Stress factors that are under the control of the individual fancier are: cold; excessive heat; dampness (chilling); lack of fresh, clean air; over-crowding; poor diet; lack of clean water; boredom; bad hygiene; and the pairing up in the breeding season before both the hen and cock are in a true breeding condition.

12
Preparing for Show

The canary show period, in the months of October, November, and December, is the grand finale of your twelve months of keeping your birds. However, if a fancier thinks that preparing for show consists of just two or three weeks of careful feeding and a few fine mist-sprays, then he has still much to learn before he can truly say that he has sent his birds out to win. To get your birds in top condition for a show, or even more importantly for several shows over a two- or three-month period, requires the assistance of an experienced fancier. You will only acquire these skills by first reading about them and then talking to your fellow fanciers who have already acquired the know-how.

The first requirement for you to achieve with your birds is an outward appearance of them being in show condition. Of this, 90 per cent is dependent solely on the fancier and his daily management, which starts with hygiene of drinkers, watering, feeding, and housing of all the birds in your bird room. Clean fresh water should be given each morning, a balanced diet continued, with fresh, crisp, green food, full of Nature's vitamins as described in earlier chapters. Remember that your birds can only eat what you give them.

Two or three mornings each week a shallow bath of clean water should be put in each bird's cage front. Those birds that do not have a bath should be given a gentle, fine mist-spray three or four times a week.

Many birds that are fed, housed, and looked after in this way require very little other conditioning. Should your birds be slow in reaching this condition, then you should give them an added vitamin supplement such as Orovite 7 (see Chapter 4).

HAND WASHING

The appearance of all kinds of type or posture exhibition canaries can be improved when they have been hand washed by an experienced fancier one week before the date of the show. It really is most important that your show team are washed in an expertly carried out way. If the smallest trace of soap is left in the bird's feathers after its wash has been completed, then those parts of its feathers will be matted or stuck together when the bird's feathers have dried out.

For those of you who have not previously tried to hand wash a canary,

Hand-washing equipment. Note the jar of vinegar. A little will remove any soap left in the feathers while being rinsed

this is how you go about it. First you require a small basin in which you can prepare your washing liquid. You can either prepare it by using a gentle-action baby shampoo, or quarter fill the basin with really hot water into which you will hold, and keep stirring, a tablet of Pears soap until it gradually dissolves. When the water in the basin becomes soapy, half fill the basin with cold water – about the same temperature as your hand. Next, take three thoroughly clean washing-up bowls and fill them three-quarters full of clean water, again at hand temperature. Place them in a row, and in the last bowl put one teaspoonful of vinegar, stirring it up well. The reason for putting the vinegar in the last bowl of rinsing water is to help to dispel any small amounts of soap that still might be present in the bird's feathers after they have been rinsed thoroughly in bowls one and two.

You will also require two old shaving brushes or two pieces of fine, soft sponge, one to use solely to apply the soapy water in the basin and the other to use in conjunction with the three bowls of rinsing water. Next you will require for each bird you are going to wash a piece of linen or old tea-cloth, some 10 cm (4 in) wide by 30 cm (12 in) long, which you will fold round the bird after the final rinse.

Finally, you will need to help the bird dry out its feathers, either in a hospital cage with an inside temperature of 30°C (85°F) or a clean show cage that has a layer of blotting-paper on the bottom, the show cage's inside to be gently heated by an electric fire. Care must be taken to ensure that the inside of the cage does not receive the fire's full heat.

We now proceed to hand washing the first bird. Catch up in your hand the bird to be washed, holding it with its chest on the palm of your hand. We can now commence the hand washing by picking up the first shaving brush or piece of sponge and dipping it into the basin of warm, soapy water. We start by first giving a soapy soak to the dirtiest parts of the bird, which are the back of the neck and the tail. While these parts are soaking commence to wash the bird. Start at the head and stroke the shaving brush along in the same direction as the feathers. The order of washing should be head, back, and wings, then turn the bird over to

Plastic mist-sprayer

wash its throat and body. Having done that, again turn the bird over in your hand and wash its neck and then its tail – supporting the tail with your wrist.

Now pick up the second shaving brush and, in the same order as before, rinse the feathers in the first bowl of water, keeping the shaving brush very wet. Next, again rinse the bird, this time in bowl number two. Now give the bird a final rinse in bowl number three, which contains the vinegar. Using a piece of linen or tea-towel, gently wipe all the surface water off the bird in the same order as you did in bowl number two.

Next, gently wrap one of the lengths of linen around the bird, leaving only its beak visible, and place it on the floor of the warm hospital or show cage. After some ten minutes in the cage, gently remove the linen wrapping, and then leave the bird for two hours in which to dry out all its feathers thoroughly. While the feathers are drying out, every ten minutes or so look to see that all is well with the bird. When it is completely dry the bird should look like Cinderella – dressed up for going to the ball, in our case a show. You can now switch off the heating, put a shallow drinker of water on the cage, and leave it overnight in the house. Return the bird to a clean stock cage the next morning.

For each of the next three days, give the bird a light, gentle spray. This will encourage it to preen all its feathers so that they rest in their own natural positions. Our Norwich canary is now ready for the show.

FEET AND LEGS

With any adult show canaries, I gently rub their legs and feet with a mixture of zinc ointment and paraffin, using my finger and thumb and at the same time wiping off any surface liquid. This helps the birds to keep an appearance of an unflighted bird and slows down any sign of ugly scales on their legs.

SHOW POINTS

With a Norwich canary its colour must be bright, rich, pure, and level throughout. The importance and skill required to colour feed your birds, both before, during, and after the moult has been stressed in Chapter 1. The head should be round, full, and neat with the actual eye visible. The face should have a good rise above the beak and have a broad appearance with no tendency to look 'mean'. Some Norwich fail in the head because of heavy feathers coming over the side of the bird's eye. It should possess a short cobby body with a well-filled-in wide back, and the chest should be full and deep, giving it a broad appearance. The neck should be short and thick, blending with the shoulders and body. The feather must be soft and silky, with brilliance and compactness, clearly showing the outline of the body. The overall size should be 15.25–16 cm (6–$6\frac{1}{4}$ in) in length and the complete bird should be well proportioned. The beak should be clear, short, and stout, the legs well set back, and the feet and nails perfect.

To assist your bird to please the judge's eye, it must be exhibited in a freshly-painted and spotlessly-clean show cage, with the cage label attached in the approved position – as shown on p. 125.

A lack of proportion in a Norwich is probably the most noticeable to anyone with an experienced eye. I find that many breeders' birds fail through poor carriage. The failure of a Norwich to display itself properly at the time it is judged can often be the reason why we sometimes see an excellent bird placed second in its class. That is why it is so vitally important that we record all the bird's faults in our breeding records. The angle to the perch is very important to the position of the bird in its show cage – the legs must be well set back. No fancier ever produces a best Norwich in show if he allows sentiment to rule his better judgement when selecting breeding pairs.

As an incorrect shape is all too frequently seen in a bird that also has incorrect carriage, and as symmetry, proportion, and carriage are so dependent on the bird having the same position on the perch, I cannot stress too strongly just how important it is to remember this when selecting your breeding pairs. Lack of attention to this is the reason why so many fanciers take many different breeding seasons before they can see an improvement in type and quality of their birds.

Always remember that with a Norwich the beauty of type can be enhanced or marred by a bird's actual carriage, and type is so dependent on its complete make-up, i.e., head, neck, body, tail and legs. It really is a most important and difficult ideal to get right but, when you have actually bred such a bird that closely resembles the ideal, then what a feeling of achievement you have!

SHOW CAGES

Dimensions

CAGE
30.5 cm (12 in) long × 29 cm (11½ in) high × 12 cm (4¾ in) broad (all outside sizes), constructed from 5-mm (3/16 in) thick timber. 30-mm (1¼-in) diameter hole on centre roof.

FRONT
Eighteen wires 6 mm (5/8 in) spacing sixteen SWG fourth wire from each end at top. Pins between third and fourth wire from each end at bottom. Drinker hole 25-mm (1-in) square central between ninth and tenth wires.

DOOR
9 cm (3½ in) diameter fitted on right-hand side hinging from rear.

PERCHES
12 mm × 9 mm or 12 mm × 12 mm (½ in × 3/8 in or ½ in × ½ in) not tipped or marked, grooved ends to fit flush on bar and seventh wire from

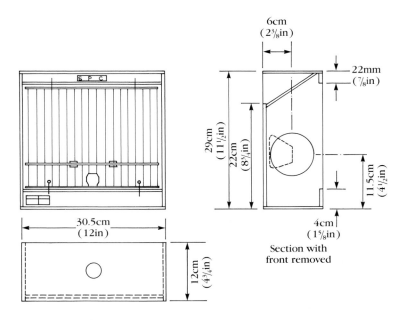

Standard Norwich show case with SPC labels and cage label in position

Norwich show cage

Norwich carrying-case and show cases

Norwich carrying-case and show cases

each side of front. Material to be of natural wood (no bleached spars allowed). It is permissible to round off sharp edges of spars.

DRINKER
Standard type zinc, all black exterior and rim, natural interior. Plastic – all black.

PAINTING
Valspar black exterior, interior nearest to Valspar Meadow Green enamel – no overlays of varnish, etc. Any obvious oddness in cage or fitments may lead to disqualification.

LABELS
SPC label on top rail *directly above drinker hole.* Cage label on bottom rail. Left-hand side, member's label if any on right-hand side.

SEED
Plain canary seed only on bottom of show cage prior to completion of judging.

JUDGES

It is an interesting point to consider as to what class of fanciers make the best all-round judges. I have frequently heard it said that no fancier can judge properly unless he has been a successful breeder of several types of canary. It is undoubtedly true that the experienced breeder possesses a substantial advantage, but in my opinion he may not possess the necessary qualities that go to make a good judge, namely, a good eye for a bird and the ability to make up his mind. I have known some of the most successful exhibitors to have been at a loss when confronted with choosing the seven best birds out of a class of fifty or more. Other judges have been unable to decide the crucial point, and have spent far too long on a single class. A good, natural judge, with perhaps less experience than a breeder, might have picked out the winner in a few minutes. Therefore it seems to me there is a very good reason for assuming that successful judges are born and not made.

However, the judge's distinctive ability to pick out good birds and decide between their merits is enhanced by practical experience of the various breeds, their characteristics, and the methods of breeding them. This is of particular importance at such outstanding shows as the British Border Fancy Canary Club held in November, where there will be an entry in excess of 2,500 Borders, and at which the champion unflighted classes will have entries of between 90 and 100 Borders *in each class.* At this kind of show only a fully-experienced judge of that particular variety of canary is competent to officiate. It is, of course, inevitable that in the awards every judge will be freely and often adversely criticised. Fanciers, as a rule, are the best of sportsmen, and accept defeat in philosophic mood, but among such a large community there are naturally a number of exhibitors who are blind to the merits of any bird but their own. They apparently forget that a judge is not in a position to share their enthusiasm but is merely required to exercise his unbiased opinion. Mistakes do, of course, occur from time to time, and I have said earlier there are times when, looking over a class for a second time, a judge may feel dissatisfied with his placings of the awards. But many so-called mistakes are merely differences of opinion, and the more experienced exhibitor knows well that unless a bird stands out head and shoulders above its fellows, he cannot expect every judge to place the same value on it.

It so happens that a good bird is sometimes passed over by a judge for no other reason than lack of show-cage training. As I have already remarked, a judge is invariably working to the clock to complete his number of classes, so if an exhibit persists in playing up while it is being judged, then the adjudicator cannot spare the time, and so that particular exhibit has to take a back seat. A Norwich turned out by a fancier who wants his exhibit to catch the judge's eye while it is on the judging bench should always remember that *he* is responsible for 80 per cent, or even more, of the exhibit's quality.

13
The Australian Experience

The following information and observations should be of interest to all breeders of Norwich canaries. They were collected on my travels to Australia and so should be of special interest to breeders in the southern hemisphere.

DIET

Colour feeding It is before moulting begins that breeders of Yorkshires and Norwich Plainheads introduce colour food to their birds. There are many lines available in pet shops for this purpose, and some breeders find them very effective. However, I use only sweet paprika to colour the soft food and I hang slices of sweet red pepper on the cage front with the other greens. After the birds have finished moulting, colour food is still given right up to show time. This is to make sure that, should a bird

Peter Rayson's canary room, which he has built in the bush in Victoria, Australia

lose a feather, the new one will come through in the same colour as the other feathers. Patchy colour spoils a bird for the show bench. If you keep Border canaries as well as the colour-fed varieties then you must make sure that they do not have any access to colour feeding – a colour-fed Border canary would be disqualified immediately on the show bench.

Collecting food Beware of plants fouled by dogs or other animals. Do not use any plant growing near a septic-tank outlet or polluted courses and drains, etc. Remove all uneaten greens, fruit, grasses, or sprouted seed daily as they can ferment easily and cause sickness very quickly. Aphids on thistles and vegetables are not harmful, in fact birds enjoy a little 'meat' with their salad.

Dry seed Use the following: canary, rape, niger, maw and crushed sunflower.

Sprouted seed Use canary seed, rape seed, sunflower seed, various millets, oats, wheat and clover seed.

Seeding grasses Use Poaannua – a winter grass; canary grass, spring and summer – a first-class food; Phalaris – in spring time hang it up in bunches to semi-dry; rye grass – to be fed in the spring time; cocksfoot – feed in the spring and the summer time; milk-thistle seed – feed when available; dandelion leaves and flowers – can be fed at all times, but the leaves should be young and tender; sow thistle (not the prickly leaves)

A typical Australian canary flight

130

Sow thistle, a very good food for feeding hens

– the seeding heads only should be used; chickweed – this can be fed when in season; knot grass – seed heads only can be fed when they are available.

Weeds Fog grass – this should not be used when feeding weeds to birds; barley grass – the same applies to this seed; wild turnip – another wild seed to be avoided; cape weed – a seed also not used in Australia. Seeding heads of millet seed, Jap, white, or Panicum are all excellent forms of food for feeding hens and growing chicks.

VEGETABLES AND FRUITS

Rape plant, the leaves, yellow flowers, and the green seed-pods are good for all birds. The tender leaves of broccoli can be fed as well as the flowers when in season. Young, tender leaves of cabbage are very good for all forms of cage birds. Brussels sprouts, providing they have not been frosted, are good for your canaries. Kale is an excellent green food and a source of iron tonic for your birds. Apples, oranges, pears, sweet corn (raw or cooked cob), and grated or boiled carrots are also good for your birds. Chinese cabbage is an excellent form of food. Spinach is equally good to use when available and given fresh. You can feed the leaves, stalks and seeding heads of silver beet. Chicory is an excellent food that is easily grown.

Salad lettuce I do not recommend, as it goes off easily and is best left

131

alone. Watercress is very good for all cage birds as well as human beings. Lucerne, chopped, green or dried, ground-up and added to soft food in small amounts is also something that should not be omitted. Nasturtium leaves and flowers should be fed during the spring and summer. Marigold seeding flower-heads can be fed primarily to colour-fed Norwich canaries. Russian comfrey (put the plant in a small container) can have its leaves chopped and fed to the birds in a soft food dish. Semi-ripe seed heads of dock are an excellent form of food for all canaries because they also contain a high percentage of oil. Many Australians feed green cucumber, and this is also good for the birds.

BOB ENNIS, QUEENSLAND

One of the most respected Norwich fanciers in Australia is Bob Ennis of Scarborough, Queensland, who has a large and very well-appointed bird room. I was impressed by the very high quality and standard of his birds. I was very interested to hear him stress the importance of the presence of green blood in his stock. He maintains the importance of this in his Norwich's quality of feather, colour, and vigour. This confirms my remarks made in Chapter 1 – and we both breed and exhibit canaries in opposite parts of the world in completely different weather conditions!

Bird room negatives
1. Do not hope to get the best birds at a cheap price. Good birds are hard to breed, so you cannot expect a breeder to sell you outstanding specimens at less than a good price. Remember he had to pay a fair price for his stock and has spent considerable time in builidng up his standard of stock, therefore good birds must always cost a little more.
2. Do not buy a bird because it is cheap unless it is the bird you are looking for. A cheap bird can be expensive at any price.
3. Do not commence with too many birds. Let quality not quantity be your guiding factor.
4. Do not buy unhealthy birds, however long their pedigree. An unhealthy bird of a weakling will assuredly breed youngsters that are not up to par or with a tendency to that weakness.
5. Do not depend on your own judgement in your purchases if you can avail yourself of advice from an experienced breeder of the variety you are choosing.
6. Do not forget to ask the breeder how the birds have been bred and fed. To know how they are bred is important for your stock-book record, and to know how they have been fed will enable you to adapt your own to that of the breeder. A sudden change of diet can cause a loss of condition.
7. Do not buy dusty seed. Always buy seed from a good source where it has been through an air-cleaning process.
8. Do not just empty the drinking containers and refill them, but wash them out well with warm water and a bottle brush, then rinse well.

9. Do not be afraid to allow plenty of fresh air into your bird room, but be sure that it does not cause draughts as this will cause bad results and problems.
10. Do not let your cages get dirty and do not leave dirty and used utensils around your room.
11. Do not pair birds if they are not in the highest condition. It is better to wait a while longer than have infertile eggs.
12. Do not expect everything to go like clockwork – some hens take longer than others to settle in.
13. Do not assume eggs are infertile if not hatched on time – occasionally the hen does not sit close for a day or two, hence hatching is a little late.
14. Do not attempt to break an egg to release a chick. If the egg has not hatched naturally it will not contain a healthy chick. The only attempt that should be made to aid hatching is to let the egg float in lukewarm water for a few seconds. Those containing a live chick will bob and kick.
15. Do not pair faults and weaknesses together – definitely out.

Positives
1. Always try to pair yellow feather to buff feather.
2. Use plastic, glass or china drinking vessels when giving any medicine or tonic.
3. Water containing medicine, etc., should be changed every day unless the prescription states otherwise.
4. Make sure food containers are checked regularly to ensure sufficient is available to the birds.
5. It is recommended to keep a supply of cuttlefish and grit in all cages.
6. When supplying birds with greens, give them fresh each day and in the forenoon.
7. Make a practice of always removing stale, green feed from cages.
8. Ensure that birds are protected from excessive heat or cold.
9. Watch out for lice, red mite, and other vermin, and take all the necessary precautions and preventive measures to eradicate.
10. When making any changes in the feeding routine or pattern, or introducing new types of food, it should be a gradual process.
11. Always try to be patient and take time and care when attending to your birds.
12. Before leaving the bird room or aviary always make sure that doors on cages are securely closed.
13. Whenever you are in doubt on any aspects of canary breeding it is advisable to consult an established fancier.
14. Do join a bird society and attend meetings as regularly as possible.
15. Do pair a cock and a hen. Two hens will give plenty of eggs – as a lot of us have found out, but they are only worth scrambling!

BILL DUNN, SOUTH AUSTRALIA

The following remarks were made by Bill Dunn, the Honorary Secretary of Adelaide Canary Society, who is a great admirer of the Norwich canary:

Much has been said here in South Australia about just what constitutes the ideal Norwich bird. Most of the comments I have heard originate from exhibitors of other varieties. I feel if one is to sound off about a variety, then prove that they are right by breeding their ideal bird and troop it around Australia. Come back with your champion awards and I for one, will listen.

There is only one specialist Norwich breeder in South Australia and he has proven his point, that is Ted Jackson. He has continually bred Norwich birds and maintained his position at the top. It is alright to win one now and again but to continue to win is the proof of the pudding. I know of many breeders who have been lucky enough to obtain culls from Ted. Perhaps they breed the odd winner, but are never able to produce winners year after year like the master.

I think most of us look at the Norwich drawing and forget to read the description of the bird using the beautiful adjectives which leaves little doubt what is required in the ideal bird.

The head of an ideal Norwich should be very thick and chubby, presenting an appearance of roundness even though it be not round. There must be no flatness about either front, top, sides or back. It should rise gracefully from the base of the beak, and fall away into the neck at its junction with the base of the skull. Viewed from the front, back or in profile, the head should have the appearance of roundness; there must be no angularity anywhere, no flatness of skull, and overhanging eyebrows. The eye should be bold and set in a line with the beak. It should be nearly in the centre of the head. The beak should be short and neat.

A typical Norwich should be short, thick and stout in neck – in a word, bull-necked. The head, neck and shoulders of a good Norwich should be bunched up together. A good-necked Norwich should have no neck. The body must be round and compact, deep through from back to breast, broad in the chest and shoulders, well rounded in front and at the sides, while the back itself should be broad and slightly rounded. From the shoulders to the tail the back should present an appearance not of flatness, nor of roundness, but of being well filled in. While the front of the body or chest requires to be bold, deep and broad, that portion behind the legs should be altogether different. Behind the legs there should be little body, and what there is should have a well cut-away appearance; the ideal Norwich is short all over.

The wings should be well set into the shoulders; they should also be short, tightly braced, and carried very close to the body. The flights must lie nice and evenly, with the tips meeting just over the root of the tail.

The tail needs to be very short, very tightly folded, and carried at a nice angle from the body, of which it should very definitely present the appearance of being a part.

A Norwich should be smart and lively in its movements, and show a reasonable jauntiness and pertness of carriage. In this connection mention should be made of the legs; they have much to do with the correct carriage of the body. If the legs are too long the body will be carried too upright and not enough across the perch. On the other hand, if they are too short the bird will look cloddy and heavy and be somewhat sluggish in its movements. With legs of medium length, the bird is able to put just sufficient boldness into its carriage to throw its chest well across the perch, and for its head to be lifted well up in a bold, fearless manner.

Having a body approaching the ideal, we want it clothed in a coat of soft, silky feather, the under flue of which should be as soft and yielding as floss silk, while the top should be firm, bright, and glistening, like a piece of highly-finished dress silk.

Colour plays a great part in judges' decisions, and always will, because nothing attracts the eye so much as a rich colour.

There is never a perfect bird, and we all see the Norwich slightly different, but firstly there must be 'type', if that is not present then it is pointless wasting your time exhibiting it.

Then the faults are discounted from the possible score, according to the judge's opinion or preferences.

ALGIE LITTLE, TASMANIA

Ever since I attended my first canary show almost twenty years ago, I have never ceased to be fascinated by the Norwich canary. To the dedicated breeders who many years ago set out to breed this bird up to the standard that we have today we owe a great deal. To set up a model with a standard set of points is one thing, but to breed the birds to the model is where the breeder's skill is tested.

Today's Norwich is a cobby, thick-set bird, beautifully rounded at all angles with a well-proportioned head with a good lift off a very short beak, a clear, well-positioned eye and close carried wings. The bird must be well filled in down the back and have a short tail nicely piped and stand well across the perch with almost 60 per cent of its body in front of the perch. For the correct stance it must have short legs set well back, showing a very small percentage of hock. This correct stance will give your bird a showy, thrustful appearance. The feathers should be fine and silky and above all else, must be well drawn underneath without evidence of loose feathers around the flank, thigh and vent areas.

Canary standards, like most live stock, are changed periodically. Today's border fancy is a much bigger bird than that of 30 years ago. Yorkshires are also bigger and heavier but the Norwich are somewhat smaller. Some breeds, unfortunately, have become extinct.

Today, this smaller breed of Norwich, still classed as one of the big breeds, is enjoying an increase in popularity. This is very good for the fancy and easy to understand as they are a very showy type bird, lend themselves well to colour feeding due to their deep intense natural colour, and are easy to breed.

Showing

For the fancier who breeds to show his birds the Norwich has several advantages over other breeds. Firstly, his show position is his natural stance, very little training is required. Secondly, by exhibiting in the English standard box-type cage, the bird can only see what it is required to see and is not easily distracted. Thirdly, this type cage offers the bird better protection than the open wire cages, during exhibitions in cold, draughty halls; and finally it is much easier to transport and not so easily damaged. In many instances travelling to exhibitions is a tiring and unpleasant experience for the owner and his birds. Some birds don't stand up to this ordeal and become listless and even lose weight. Norwich canaries due to their stamina and the advantages of their cages, as previously mentioned usually show no ill effect from such experiences and a smaller team to select one's birds from need only be kept in show condition.

In all forms of livestock breeding the natural tendency is to set a high value on size, that there should be a difference of opinions, and so we use our model as a yard stick, a different degree of value when showing the birds on the show bench. That is why we endeavour to select the one we think resembles the model when preparing our show team. Personally, I believe in the old saying that a good big one will always beat a good small one.

After a few seasons on the show circuit a breeder, if he or she is observant enough, can often visualise what type of bird a certain judge will select as his winner and so select birds to their liking. I have strong feelings that one should be a specialist breeder and promote the breed of your choice at all times.

Cinnamons

The Norwich breeder has the added advantage that if he wishes to try his skills at colour breeding, there is the Norwich cinnamon. What a delightful bird this fellow is. The origin of this bird has been the subject of various theories. The attractiveness of the plumage colour, although somewhat sombre on the buff-coloured bird, seems to grow on one. The yellow bird of this variety is a true charmer. The under-feathering is very dense and a dark grey colour. The standard is very similar to the Plainhead with 25 points given for type and 30 points for colour. Pink eyes are another distinctive characteristic of the cinnamon.

The introduction of green blood into this variety increases the natural colour and also helps to maintain size in the breed.

Harold Heath's canary room and flights in Victoria, Australia

ERIC MADDISON, VICTORIA

While I was in Melbourne in November 1987, I went to see Eric Maddison, that very well-known and respected 'interstate' Norwich and Crested breeder and exhibitor. It was then their mid-canary breeding season, and Eric's birds were busy bringing up nests of young Norwich. I should at this stage tell you that Eric is now in his mid-eighties, going blind in both eyes, and can only slowly move about with the aid of a pair of crutches. Even so handicapped, his big interest in life is still his Norwich.

During the last twenty breeding seasons his canaries had had very few clear or infertile eggs, and Eric says that this is due to him trimming back all the feathers around their vents except for the guide feather. The tail feathers are cut to only half their length – a point that Eric considers is very necessary with all Norwich breeding pairs. Eric's Norwich are held in high respect by all breeders and exhibitors, state-wide for their bold heads and good rise of feather above the beak, compact bodies, and their excellent position on the perch while in a show cage. All his stock have an in-bred perfection of wing and tail carriage.

Eric recalled a meeting of the Victoria State Norwich Club held in June 1978 in Melbourne that I had attended. Harold Heath, the club President, stood up and in his hand he held two sheets of paper. He then welcomed me to the meeting, held out his two sheets of paper on which he had written some twenty-six questions 'for Joe to answer!' This was quickly enjoyed by all present, and he asked me the first question. When all the twenty-six questions had been answered, Eric Maddison stood up and said that it had been the most enjoyable Norwich Club meeting he had attended for the last twenty years!

The State of Queensland is so vast that the state Norwich Club President, Bob Innes, to enable him to carry out all his judging and show commitments, has to fly his own twin-engine airplane to cover the distance involved. I have never heard of any UK club president ever having to do the same thing.

While attending a state canary seminar two re-occurring problems were discussed at some length, and a very effective remedy to them was found. The first was egg binding. It was explained in detail that this problem with some hens was entirely due to that particular hen's body organism lacking calcium. To avoid this happening to your birds, on pairing up your breeding birds and until a full clutch of eggs has been laid, you should put three or four drops of liquid calcium in each pair of birds' drinking water daily. This can be obtained from any veterinary surgeon.

However, during the breeding season, should one of your hens become egg bound, the remedy is simple and very effective. Catch up the affected hen and, holding her in your hand by her shoulders, open the beak wide and put down her throat one drop of liquid calcium, and then put her in a warm hospital cage. After only a short while she will have completed the laying of the egg, and she can be returned to her breeding cage, when it will be found that she will complete the laying of her clutch of eggs.

The second problem was a canary that had feather lice or mite. The most effective, completely harmless way, was again to catch up the affected bird, and to dust all its feathers thoroughly with pyrethum powder. Then, using your finger tips, gently work the powder down to the bird's skin. Just one such treatment will kill off all the mite or lice. It is a much more effective way than using anti-mite spray as this will quickly run off the feathers – any that might not do so is quickly dispelled into the air by the bird's naturally-high body temperature.

CAROLINE AND MANOU CHEMLAL, WESTERN AUSTRALIA

Caroline and Manou Chemlal regularly breed over 250 young canaries each year. 'Green food causes diarrhoea' – fallacy. It goes without saying that all green food must be fresh, clean, and free of chemical sprays. If it is, and you provide the type of green food that your birds like best (and they are readily available) your birds should never develop diarrhoea, no matter how much they eat. Diarrhoea is a sign of inflammation of the intestinal tract, and will never be caused by fresh, clean, natural food.

'Green food should not be given to hatchlings in the first few days' – fallacy. There is no reason to withhold, and every reason to give, newly-hatched canaries green food. We have proved that they thrive and grow much better if fed green food daily. Reluctant feeders among parents are frequently stimulated to feed better by a tempting piece of fresh green food. We have never observed a single adverse effect on any hatchlings – quite the reverse. Our youngsters receive fresh greens two or three times a day.

'Breeding canaries are easily disturbed' – fact. Some hens will desert their eggs or young if too frequently disturbed; others will sit tight on the nest and neglect to feed. A fright caused by loud noises of bumps, or a change of cage or nest position, can have the same effect. Canaries appreciate peace and privacy when breeding.

'Young birds should not be weaned till at least thirty days old' – fallacy. All living things are programmed for reproductive cycles of multiples of seven. Thus, canary eggs take fourteen days to hatch, and canary young take twenty-one days to reach weaning age. At that point they are capable, if healthy, of looking after themselves, no matter how much they appear to need their parents' attention. The hen, too, at this point, is ready to go to nest again and wants to be rid of them. She may well pluck her young for fresh nesting material if they are left with her.

'Small hens make better mothers' – fact. In general this is true, given an optimum state of health in each bird. Possibly this is because a small hen is naturally more lively, and so less likely to become over fat and lazy. The smaller varieties are closest, both in size and breeding, to the original, and therefore more likely to retain their natural instincts to a greater degree.

'Frequent showing of canaries damages the birds' nervous system and spoils them for breeding' – fallacy. The fancier's nervous system is much more likely to be damaged by a frequent showing than the actual bird's. Always provided birds are healthy and receiving regular optimum nutrition, they are in no way injured by going to shows. In fact it can be good for them, they become more used to activity around them, and therefore more steady in the show cage and also during the breeding season.

Glossary of Terms

Action Refers to a canary's movement while on the perch of a show cage.

Buff The term used when a bird's feather at the extreme tip carries little colour.

Carriage The bearing and position on the perch in a show cage.

Cell A minute, basic, unit of a living matter.

Chromosomes Microscopic gene-carrying bodies in the tissue of a cell, formed before cell divisions take place. The XX and XY chromosomes indicate a bird's sex, where the XX is carried by the cock and XY by the hen.

Clear A bird whose feathers have no melanistic colour at all.

Dominant character When a breeding pair of canaries produce young ones which outwardly show the characteristics of one parent, then that parent's genes are dominant to the other parent's genes.

Fertile When a canary produces functional gene cells.

Fertilisation The union of male and female sperm on copulation.

Flighted A bird that is over one-year-old and has moulted out its tail and wing feathers.

Flights The primary quills or long outer feathers in the wing.

Genes Microscopic hereditary-carrying factors for such features as colour, sex, feather quality, size, and so on.

Genetics A combination of two dominant factors, often referred to as the art of canary breeding.

Grizzle Feathers that are streaked and intermingled, which intensifies the finish of the feathers.

Ground colour The general colour of the body feathers.

Heredity Where there is a pronounced tendency of an organism to transmit its nature or likeliness to its young.

Inheritance Features obtained from parent birds.

Long-in-the-barrel A term used to describe a Norwich that is too long in the body.

Melanins The black and brown pigments on buff-coloured birds, formed from proteins produced by a bird, and which are carried in the bloodstream to the feathers at moulting time.

Mutation A spontaneous change in the structure of a gene.

Ovary The female reproductive gland. It should be noted that hens also have Fallopian tubes.

Overshown A bird that has been exhibited at too many shows, with the result that it is tired, has lost some of its show sparkle, and hence feather quality is lacking.

Pencilling The narrow lines of darker-coloured feathers on the back and sides in self-greens and cinnamons.

Position The carriage of a bird when in a show cage.

Quality An attribute to a bird's feather, condition, colour, and type.

Recessive Can be described as negative recessive genes carried by a bird.

Saddle That part of the back behind the shoulders.

Self A term applied to greens and cinnamons which have no light-coloured feathers at all.

Sex chromosomes Where the cock can only carry XX chromosomes and the hen carries XY chromosomes it is the hen who determines the sex of a chick.

Soft A feather indication that a bird is not its normal healthy self.

Stamina Indicates a bird's health, strength, and vigour.

Steady A term used to indicate a bird's behaviour in a show cage. Norwich canaries are noted for their very relaxed and steady nature.

Strain Normally is associated to one particular fancier's birds, who are all very similar to each other in type and feather, and are all directly blood related.

Tailing When all the tail feathers of a nest-feather bird are removed.

Thick set Refers to the shape of the body. All Norwich canaries must have a stout-built appearance, with the neck in proportion to the body, and the neck must be a fully-blended part of the body. No visible sign of a ruffle between neck and body.

Ticked A bird with only one dark mark that can be covered by a one-pence coin, or that has not more than three dark feathers that are side-by-side in either the tail or one wing. The bird otherwise has clear, unmarked feathers.

Type The overall characteristic of a bird that resembles the standard of excellence, in this case that of a Norwich.

Unflighted A current-year bird, one that has not moulted its tail or flight feathers.

Variegated Birds that have more light than dark feathers.

Index

Note: page numbers in *italics* refer to illustrations.